Do Something Different...
For a Change

An Insider's Guide to What Your
Therapist Knows

(But May Not Tell You)

Persevere!

Peggy Mitchell Norwood, PhD

Peggy Mitchell Norwood

Living Well Press, LLC
Denver, CO 80207 USA

Published by Living Well Press, LLC
Denver, CO 80207
www.livingwellpress.com

*Do Something Different...For a Change: An Insider's Guide to
What Your Therapist Knows (But May Not Tell You)*
© 2008 by Peggy Mitchell Norwood
ISBN: 978-0-9817225-0-4

Requests for information should be directed to:
drpeg@hotmail.com
Visit www.DrPegOnline.com

Cover design by RNR Design Group

Printed in the United States of America

*This book is dedicated to
my children, Ali and Richard,
the best kids
a mother could ever wish for.*

Acknowledgements

I thank God for giving me a dream and the desire to write. Oh, that He would bless me indeed!

There have been so many individuals who have encouraged, helped, supported, and inspired me. A heartfelt thank you goes out to my many friends, family, and colleagues who each, in his or her own way, contributed to the writing and publication of this book. I'd especially like to thank my friends who purchased advance copies of my book. Your support and confidence mean so much!

A very special thank you to Susan Achziger, Dr. Linda Bradford, Debra Bryson, Rosalina Blanc, Caroline Brodie, Dawn Bryant, Linda Buzogany, Marian Carrington, Dr. Kevin Cook, Dr. Michele Cooley-Strickland, Jay Devaughn, Darryl Dodson, Wayne Figueira, Kay Franklin, Keith Frazier, Kim Freeman, Dr. Johanna Gallers, Pastor Toni Graham, Marvela Guice, Michael Hernandez, Jr., Holly Hinderlie, Dr. Nancy Jackson, Elaine Jacobs, Susie Jacobs, Pastor Antwan Jefferson, Dr. Sheri Johnson, Jolianne and Paul Jones, Regina Joyner, Jacki Kimble-Beder, Irene King, Lynn and Cecile Lantz, Leland Melvin, Lisa Mickey, Pastor Kay Michaelis, Karen McMullen, Romalia Mitchell, Winston and Rose Nurse, Pam Patterson, Marva Pattillo, Tilloretta Pope, Richard Rhodes, Sheridan Samano, Chet Sisk, David and Cynthia Smith, Pastor Phil Smith, Jeri Steen, Kathryn Stoker, Whitney Traylor, Carla Washington, Shelley Wood, and Laura Wright.

To Daddy, I wish I could have done something different.

To Mommy, More, and Pete, let's do something different now!

do | doō | verb

perform, work on; solve; produce; achieve; complete;
finish

something | ˈsəm͵ θ i ng | pronoun

a thing that is unspecified or unknown

different | ˈdif(ə)rənt | adjective

fresh; novel; new; not the same as another

for a

change | ch ā nj | noun

the substitution of one thing for another; an alteration or
modification; a new or refreshingly different experience;
the act or instance of making or becoming different

CONTENTS

A Message from
Dr. Michele Cooley-Strickland

Our society's technological ability to connect to others surpasses any previous generation, yet we have amazingly become increasingly isolated. We are disconnected from our families, friends, communities, nations, ourselves, and God. *Do Something Different...For a Change* helps facilitate connectedness, beginning with our inner selves. Reading this book "interactively," as Dr. Peg recommends, makes change possible—even probable—with limitless possibilities.

As part of the exercises to help deepen the growth process, Dr. Peg suggests creating a small group to study with others. Given the significance of change and the power of groups, I strongly recommend this book for Book Clubs. The human exchange provided therein leads to truth, accountability, and wholeness—with the proper tool to facilitate it. *Do Something Different...For a Change* is that very tool.

Take the challenge. Take the journey. By virtue of your scanning the title and picking up this book, you've demonstrated that you are indeed ready for a change. Read *Do Something Different...* tonight, and have a better tomorrow.

Dr. Michele Cooley-Strickland is a Licensed Psychologist and Associate Professor at Johns Hopkins Bloomberg School of Public Health

Foreword by
Dr. Johanna Gallers

Not another self-help book on *change*! Are there really any readers out there who don't already have one or even several such tomes on their bookshelves, collecting dust? The reason there are so many self-help-change books is because our behavior is something we talk about changing, but don't.

We've heard that change is really difficult and that it takes 21 days to create a new habit, as well as lose an old one. So why is change so daunting? We are programmed not to change. Only we don't know it. The media, our therapists, parents and friends instruct us to think *new and different*: get a new car, a new washing machine, a new face, a new personality, new friends and even a new partner—that's the American way.

We go out and buy self-help books that promise to teach us how to live up to our social and civic responsibilities to remake ourselves. And we fail because we still don't understand the mysteries of human nature.

I studied the psycho-biology of change and learned that humans come hard-wired for six basic emotions: fear (the biggie), anger, sadness, startle reaction and disgust, on the negative side, with pleasure bringing up the rear as the only positive or happy emotion. No wonder we have so much difficulty making different choices; there is a lot of internal pressure to stay in our little ruts.

But making peace with our internal world is just the start. Not only are humans genetically predisposed to resist change, I learned, but cultures are, too. If you look at the bell curve, which represents how the populace of countries or cultures naturally assemble themselves, you'll see that on any dimension of behavior, 95% of the population is within two standard deviations of the mean. Most humans don't wander far behaviorally from the mean, which represents socially acceptable behavior.

Oh, society gives us some leeway to change; we can make small changes with society's blessing. But it's clear that big changes come at a cost, the price being social disapproval. A person, for example, can move to a new place, but once he gets there he may find that making friends and fitting in is difficult because there is already an established social hierarchy. Social upheaval threatens social stability, so it is in the culture's best interest for members today to tread well-worn paths.

The obstacles to change, then, seem insurmountable. Does this mean humans are doomed? No, it just means that we need to understand how difficult it is *to* change and plan accordingly—which brings me back to this book and why it is different from other self-help books on change.

Dr. Norwood gets it. She's not offering up seven easy steps to infinite wisdom. She's telling us that change is hard and that we have to work at learning different behaviors and keep on working at those behaviors until we build new pathways in our brains so that the new behaviors are as automatic as the old ones. Change, she reminds us, is not a function of other people's insights and words, but a function of our will to understand what behaviors work for us and what behaviors don't.

Many other self-help books on change are written by therapists who claim to be experts in the field of behavior management. We are told we should listen to them because they have treated thousands of clients and have arrived at their conclusions about what works and what doesn't from years of helping people try to change. *I am an authority on change,* they seem to be saying.

Dr. Norwood has years of experience as a therapist as well. However, she says that relying on so-called *experts* can rob us of the will to change because therapists, like the rest of society, have a vested interest in maintaining the status quo—the longer a client stays stuck, the more money a therapist makes.

The bottom line then, is that change is difficult because we get conflicting messages from society, therapists and our families. Go ahead and change, but only a little bit. If you change too much, you'll disturb the social order, you'll disrupt your therapist's income flow, and you'll upset the homeostatic balance of your relationships. Dr. Norwood understands this dilemma and she tells us that while change *is* difficult, even painful, that if we work at it and embrace the struggle, we *can* make different choices for ourselves. Despite our genetic predispositions to see the glass as half empty and despite negative social reinforcements, humans have the capacity to self-actualize. Whether we make changes or not, is up to us.

Dr. Johanna Gallers is a Clinical Psychologist in Denver, Colorado.

Prologue

One day, after thirteen years of marriage, my husband abruptly, but not totally out of the blue, announced he was moving out.

I was sitting at the computer, typing a draft of this book. I was feeling excited about how it was developing when he walked into the room and began speaking. I looked up from the computer and saw two mismatched duffel bags, one in each of his hands.

He started calmly, "I'm not happy, and I don't think you're happy." Most of what he said is a blur now, but I'm sure it wasn't anything I hadn't heard him say many times before. I interrupted, resigned to where I knew this was going. His attempt to soften the blow had created a palpable tension.

"What are you trying to say?" I asked. "Just cut to the chase."

More words from him; most of it is also a blur. By the end of the evening, my husband was gone.

Just the night before, I had come to the painful realization that my marriage had fallen apart. I felt totally disconnected from my husband. I cried out to God with some difficult questions.

"What do I need to do? How can I fix this?" I asked.

The answer I heard in my heart surprised me: "Do nothing. Be kind, gentle, tenderhearted, patient, and forgiving. Otherwise, there's nothing more for you to do."

"Whoa!" I thought. "Do nothing? There must be some mistake!"

This would be drastically different from anything I had already been doing. Maybe I was missing the point. Perhaps the point was not so much to do nothing. Rather, the point was to do something different. I had tried so many things to fix my marriage that, in my case, doing nothing was tantamount to doing something different. The irony was not lost on me. In the midst of writing a book called *Do Something Different...For a Change*, I clearly knew that I myself needed to do something different.

I began to study every concept and recommendation in this book. Like an expert diamond cutter, I examined my current situation through the lens of my own words. I looked at each difficulty in my life and planned how I would apply the principles in this book to the beautiful diamond that I believed my life could still become.

Diamond cutters must determine the best way to cut a rough stone to produce the most beauty and profit. The stone can be left at its maximum weight, losing much of its brilliance and sparkle, or it can be cut down much smaller into a more beautiful diamond.

Life's adversities provide opportunities to cut away the things that keep you from becoming the best possible person you can be. To achieve your true brilliance, you must be willing to go through this process.

Don't get me wrong. I'm certainly not suggesting that I needed to cut my husband out of my life in order to shine. That was the last thing I wanted. But difficult circumstances can serve as the pressure that's needed to take an ordinary rock and form it into a radiant diamond.

That pressure began several years into our marriage. We started out happy. In the thirteen years of our marriage, we had many wonderful times. We produced two beautiful children. But over the course of time, like so many couples, we became distant and disconnected emotionally.

Stormie Omartian has an interesting story in her book, *The Power of Praying Together.*[1] One morning, she was writing at her desk. The chapter was about the importance of praying for others. Much to her frustration, a man was working high up in a tree outside of her window. Because

---

[1] Stormie Omartian and Jack Hayford, *The Power of Praying Together: Where Two or More Are Gathered* (Eugene, Ore.: Harvest House Publishers, 2003).

he was making such a racket, she found it difficult to concentrate on her writing.

The disruption was making her angry and annoyed, but she had a thought. Maybe he was not making all that noise in the tree to keep her from writing her chapter on prayer. Maybe she was writing about prayer at that very moment so she could pray for him and keep him from falling.

At this point in my life, I had also ended "up in a tree," feeling broken, empty, and disconnected. Perhaps writing about doing something different at the very time my marriage was ending was precisely what I needed to keep myself from falling. Perhaps now, I even have the insight and skills to get myself safely down from the tree altogether.

So here I am, writing these words just two weeks after realizing I was up in a tree. I feel confident I will do something different to heal my emotional pain and emptiness and experience change that lasts. I'll let you know how it turns out!

About This Book

Have you ever seen a self-help book on display at the bookstore, skimmed through it, and decided it was good enough to buy? You may already have several good books sitting on your shelf at home right now. But, out of all of these books, how many have you read all the way through? It may seem obvious, but, in order for this book to help you, you must read it. More importantly, take your time and read it interactively.

With so many people talking on cell phones in public places, I can't help listening to their conversations. Have you ever tried to listen to a one-sided conversation? It goes something like this:

"So what happened after you told him you know he's been cheating with your best friend?"

Silence.

"Really? Oh my goodness! I can't believe he said that!"

I want to yell to the woman in the next bathroom stall: "What did he say? What happened next?"

Passively reading this book is the equivalent of a one-sided conversation. There's no give-and-take and a great deal of information is lost. Don't eavesdrop on the dialogue that is taking place in this book. To encourage you to read attentively and interactively, I will ask you *reflection questions*. These are intended as conversation-starters.

These questions are also designed to prompt you to deeply examine your automatic patterns of thinking, feeling, responding, and relating. The questions will have the greatest impact if you follow three recommendations:

- Be honest with yourself.
- Keep a journal.
- Share with at least one other person.

Answering the questions honestly paves the way to lasting change. Lying to yourself keeps you stuck in the very patterns that prevent you from changing. Acknowledging the truth frees you to change.

Journaling is a valuable tool for being honest. It allows you to vent your thoughts in a safe and confidential way. It provides distance from the intensity of overwhelming emotions. It imposes order and clarity on jumbled thoughts. Most significantly, journaling is a record of all of your progress. You will overcome your difficulties and prevail by regularly recounting your experiences. Seeing in writing where you were helps you recognize how far you've come.

I also encourage you to find at least one other person with whom you can share your reflection questions. Sharing your reflections will provide you with accountability, validation, and insight. You might also consider starting a small group to study this book with others.

I love courtroom dramas. Usually, the climax comes when the accused sits on the witness stand and tells what happened from his or her perspective. Nothing is more dramatic than hearing a story in the first-person. It provides a truth that you can't come by any other way. This book includes *I-witness testimonies*. The I-witness testimonies are vignettes about real people and contain excerpts from the person's own writings or journal entries. Some of their names have been changed to protect their privacy.

The I-witness testimonies demonstrate that you are not alone. Other people have the same struggles, emotions, thoughts, and reactions that you have. You might feel you're the only one, but it helps to know that others have suffered similarly and succeeded in dealing with their trying circumstances.

Not only does reading about real people who have overcome difficult situations give you hope, it may also provide a template for a solution. When you see how they address and resolve their concerns, you can identify with all or part of their solutions.

What to Expect

I know firsthand how it feels to be stuck in a rut and I have experienced deep pain in my life. I've written this book to share what I've learned from my personal experience and work as a psychotherapist with hundreds of clients over many years. I care about what happens to you. I want you to experience lasting change. Throughout this book, I will continually challenge you to be honest with yourself and do something different.

The first chapter contains an overview of the foundational principles relating to pain, suffering, and change. Chapters two through four explore the barriers to change. In chapters five through eight, I reveal what your therapist knows about therapy and behavioral change, but may not tell you. Finally, chapters nine through twelve give you the

19

principles you need to experience and maintain the change you desire.

This is a short book. It is not complicated. You can read it tonight and then wake up and do something different for a change. Are you ready? Sure you are. Let's go.

PART ONE

Chapter One
Time to Get Out of BED

Are you having trouble in your relationships? Do you feel anxious or depressed? Have you ever felt like your life was missing direction or purpose? My experience as a psychotherapist has shown me that discontentment usually stems from three core issues. You feel

- **B**roken,
- **E**mpty, or
- **D**isconnected.

That is, you are "in BED." Think about it. If, for example, you were abused as a child, you may feel broken. If you are sad or depressed, a part of you feels empty. If you struggle with loneliness, you feel disconnected.

As difficult as it is, being in BED is a part of being human. Cartoonist Jennifer Berman created a cartoon that pictures a huge auditorium at the *Adult Children of Normal Parents Annual Convention*.[2] One guy is sitting there all alone.

It's such a cliché to say you come from a dysfunctional family. It is nearly impossible to raise a child without doing something that will hurt him or her emotionally. It's not about blaming your parents. No matter who your parents are, you will experience these things to one degree or another in childhood and adulthood.

Some of us get broken more than others. For different reasons, we may end up feeling empty or disconnected. But, in time, these feelings usually subside, and you get out of BED.

If that's true, how do people end up BED-ridden and stuck in a painful, emotional rut? The very things you do to

---

[2] Jennifer Berman, *Adult Children of Normal Parents: Annual Convention and Other Cartoons* (Pocket Books, 1994).

try to get out of BED or protect yourself from being hurt in the first place don't work. They actually make you feel even worse. Your failed solutions perpetuate your pain and cause you to become BED-ridden. Your failed solutions will also cause you to suffer.

What does suffering look like? The following characteristics will help you recognize suffering:

- It is out of proportion to the initial event.
- It lingers long after the initial event.
- It is usually triggered automatically and outside of conscious awareness.
- It is based on wrong thinking, distorted ideas, and/or false assumptions about what is happening.

Sad things happen in life. Bad things occur. And you can't always do something about it. Because you can't change what has already happened to you, obviously and thankfully, your hope for relieving your suffering rests in what you are or are not doing now. Antoinette's story illustrates the connection between suffering and a failed solution to being in BED.

I-Witness Testimony: Antoinette's All Alone

I've been surviving alone for as long as I can remember. I was alone with my family, alone with my friends, and alone in a room full of people. Worst of all, I was alone in my heart and in my mind. I hated having no one to talk to, no one to hold my hand or hug me, and no one to tell me that everything's going to be okay. I hated throwing tantrums with no one to stop me or help me learn how to stop. All I've ever wanted was to be close with someone and feel as if I wasn't alone.

Antoinette suffered from the eating disorder of bulimia for almost twenty years. She would frantically binge on large quantities of fast food, pizza, ice cream, cookies, and cake. She would then drink a gallon of water to stimulate vomiting and soften the rough edges of the food as it came up. From the age of sixteen to thirty-five she did this up to six times a day. She often didn't even need to use her finger to vomit. She would just bend over the toilet and will herself to do so. The two times she was pregnant slowed her down a bit, but she still did not stop.

Antoinette will tell you that her bulimia had nothing to do with food or weight. She just as easily could have gotten into drugs or promiscuous sex as a teenager. She came to realize that she was binging and purging to take control of the desperate feelings of loneliness she experienced all of her life. She felt empty and disconnected.

Her solution was to focus her attention on her body and weight. She believed that if she were skinny enough, she would be accepted and would not feel alone anymore. This failed solution—that is, what she did in response to being in BED—actually caused her to suffer from a painful, life-long struggle with bulimia and exacerbated her feelings of emptiness and disconnectedness.

Granted, Antoinette's story is extreme, but the principle is clear. When your attempts to address being in BED fail, you will add new problems on top of your already existing distress.

So how do you get out of BED? How do you avoid suffering? How do you get unstuck? You have to fix what really needs fixing. And you have to do something different. It might be painful at times, but this is exactly what you must do if you want to experience lasting change in your life. I'm sure you'll agree that you can't keep doing things the same way and expect different results. How can you have something different if you fail to do something different? The remainder of this book will explain what you will need to do. All you have to do is do it.

If you are like most people, one thing will get in your way. You won't want to do what you already know you ought to do. Why? Doing something different is hard. It's scary, and it comes at a cost. Be encouraged. Despite these barriers, you can do something different for a change. Keep reading. I'll show you how.

Reflection Questions

Ponder the following questions. You might even want to keep a journal with your thoughts and/or start a small group and share your answers.

In what areas of your life are you broken, empty and/or disconnected?

What would your life look like if you did something different? Be specific.

What is stopping you?

Chapter One Power Points

- If you are alive, you will experience being "in BED," that is, being broken, empty, or disconnected.
- Suffering is caused by your failed solutions to being in BED.
- Change is hard and scary, and it comes at a cost.
- Do something different...for a change!

Chapter Two
Change Is Scary

In our culture, fear and horror are best-selling commodities. Halloween, including its haunted houses, ghosts, skeletons, and black cats, delights children of all ages. Who hasn't enjoyed seeing a movie that puts you on the edge of your seat? Right after you scream with horror, you giggle with glee.

But, if you mention the word "change," nobody laughs. The fear you enjoy in a dark theater becomes a paralyzing obstacle in the light of real life. Winston experienced just how paralyzing fear can be.

I-Witness Testimony: What If Winston Weren't Afraid?

I ambled into the bathroom and looked groggily in the mirror. What a handsome fellow! I turned on the shower and waited for it to come up to the proper temperature. I stepped into the shower and stood with my face and head under the overhead spray. As I stood with the water running over my head and shoulders, I heard an inaudible voice in my head saying, "Take the VRIF." VRIF is an acronym for Voluntary Reduction in Force, one of the vehicles my company was using to reduce manpower.

I wish I could say that I jumped out of the shower, ran to work, and told my boss I was quitting, but that is not what happened. Instead, I stood in the shower and tried to convince myself why quitting now was not a good idea. I loved my job. I was successful. I was not old enough to retire. I was getting a decent salary, and, besides, where would I get another job at my age? This is just not the right time, I told myself.

"My job has announced a VRIF, a voluntary reduction in force," I told my daughter Rosealine and her husband while visiting them at their home in Boston. Rosealine leaned forward, placed her elbow on her knee, and supported her chin with her hand. Then she said in a

casual, nonchalant way, as if speaking to no one, "What would you do if you weren't afraid?"

Startled, I looked at Rosealine and thought of the wisdom she had just whispered. This was confirmation that I needed to leave, but I let it pass by; I did not take the VRIF. I would later discover that the opportunity to leave at the top of my game was gone.

Not long after, I was being victimized by micro-management, and things got worse and worse. Political maneuvering and deceitfulness were rampant. I received the worst employee satisfaction survey of my career. The VP who had always been cordial to me treated me like I was week-old, un-refrigerated, dead fish. The company I once loved was the company I now loathed.

I could have sprayed blame around like bullets, aiming at upper-management, my peers, and my team members for my predicament and horrible situation. I felt persecuted. But I knew why I was being persecuted. I should have left this company several months earlier when the VRIF was offered, but I was too afraid.

Winston's company was looking to downsize and offered the VRIF as a friendly way out. After the volunteers departed, far too many workers were remaining. Once the VRIF opportunity was gone, Winston was targeted to leave. Then his career plummeted. You may have found yourself in a similar situation at work or even a relationship and wondered, "Why is this happening to me?"

In truth, Winston's situation was the inevitable, downstream consequence of fear. If he hadn't been too afraid to leave when the VRIF was first offered, he would not have been there to be on the receiving end of his employers' attempts to force him out.

Take a look at some of the problems you are facing. It might seem that things are happening to you for no apparent reason or people are simply out to get you. But, if you examine the events leading up to your situation, you will discover that fear has been a significant contributing, if not causal, factor. You were too afraid to either say no or yes. The next section will examine the reasons why you might be afraid to do something different.

The Valley of Shadows: The Unknown

When you were a small child, were you ever afraid to go to sleep alone in your room at night? Did you worry about what you thought might be hiding under your bed, in the closet, or just outside the closed door? If you definitely knew that nothing was there, would you have been able to sleep? The possibility that something could be there, that is, the uncertainty of the unknown, produced your fear.

Think back to your favorite horror movies. Consider the woman walking through the house, looking around every corner. She is terrified because of what she doesn't know or see. Where is the prank caller calling from? Is her boyfriend the axe murderer? Is that body lying on the ground really dead?

One of the biggest causes of fear is the unknown or unseen. This is especially true when you believe the unknown or unseen is dangerous or likely to result in pain or punishment. When your mind has no conception of what is in front of you, it generates the unpleasant emotion of fear. You will be reluctant to walk into what you can't see or visualize.

I've Never Done That Before: The Unfamiliar

What if you can see perfectly what's ahead of you? There is no uncertainty about it, but it is something you've never done before. Being in unfamiliar territory is scary.

I once wanted to go down the big slide at the swimming pool. I was not a strong swimmer, so I was afraid to go zooming down. There were no unknown variables. Plenty of kids were going down the slide. Nobody drowned. Did I mention I was thirty-nine years old at the time? I was afraid because I had never done it before.

31

I eventually did go down the big slide. I didn't want my kids to see their mom afraid to do something so simple just because she had never done it before. So, in the interest of serving as a role model for my children, I grit my teeth, marched up that big slide, and screamed the whole way down. When I stood up in the water, it only came up to my knees. Imagine how silly I felt afterwards for being so afraid.

The Bark That's Worse Than the Bite: What-if Thinking

Okay, so it's not unknown, and it's not unfamiliar. You know what it requires; you've even done it before. But you think to yourself, "What if something bad happens this time? What if I embarrass myself? What if it doesn't go as expected?"

You could ask yourself what-if questions until it results in mental confusion and paralysis. Imagining what could happen is usually worse than what is actually likely to happen. One strategy to uncover this unlikelihood and put your situation in its proper perspective is to ask yourself, "And then what?" Follow that up with the question, "How likely is that to actually happen?"

You will be surprised where you end up when you are willing to ask these two simple, logical questions. Here's an example:

"I better not go for that promotion. What if I don't get it?"

"And then what?"

"Everyone will think I'm a loser."

"And how likely is that to actually happen?"

"Not likely. I have several friends on the job."

"And then what?"

"They might even put in a good word for me with the boss."

When you combat fear with a sound mind and rational thinking, you'll be on your way to producing the change you want.

What If I Actually Succeed: Getting What You Want Is Scary

What happens when you finally get everything you've been working for? Once you achieve your future success, you will have so many new, exciting, and different things to enjoy. Or do you see it as so many new things to have to learn and master? And what if you blow it? Getting what you want is scary.

Achieving success will require you to operate in a realm that is unfamiliar and unknown. These two elements make change scary. When you are engaging in the new behaviors that your success demands, you may feel out of place. You may believe that everyone around you can tell you are unsure of what you are doing. You may feel inadequate compared to the other successful people around you. What if they whisper behind your back and laugh at you? That is an uncomfortable feeling.

What if you do blow it? What if they do laugh at you? You succeed. You get everything you want. And then you make a huge mistake that ruins it all. How likely is that to actually happen? And if it did, then what? The first time down the big slide is scary. But, after the first time, it gets easier. And it usually isn't as bad as you think it will be.

What If It Doesn't Satisfy Me: Getting What You Want Might Be Unfulfilling

Are you afraid you might get everything you always hoped for only to discover that it does not satisfy you the way you thought it would? Do you fear that, even with success, you won't feel good enough or you will still feel empty?

You might have believed that being successful would be the key to feeling better about yourself and healing your BED issues. But tying your identity and self-esteem to your success is a double-edged sword. When things go well, you will feel good about yourself. But, when things go poorly, you will feel bad about yourself. Even when you achieve success, why do you eventually still feel empty?

You will always feel empty when your value is tied to what you do and not who you are. Filling up with only outcome-based performance will always leave you feeling empty. It is more effective to focus on your effort rather than feeling good only about the outcome. I'll come back to this point later.

Martyrs and Drama and Fears, Oh My!

You may also fill your emptiness with excitement. If you thrive on highly emotional, unexpected events or you are at a loss for what to do with yourself when things are quiet and peaceful, you will struggle with getting what you want and not being satisfied.

There is always a letdown after something exciting happens. Achieving the success you've worked for is an amazing feeling. Once you come down from that high, you are at risk of feeling empty again. Fearing the letdown or unfamiliarity of success or not feeling fulfilled are all obstacles to doing something different for a change. I'll show you how to handle these obstacles in the third part of this book.

Reflection Questions

Not all what-if questions are bad. One good what-if question is, "What would you do if you weren't afraid?"

What would you stop doing if you weren't afraid?

Chapter Two Power Points

- The unknown is scary.
- The unfamiliar is scary.
- What-if thinking is a barrier to change.

Chapter Three
Change Is Hard

Change is hard. If it were easy, you'd already have done it. You've probably heard the saying, "Anything worth having is worth working for." You may have also heard, "No pain, no gain." Change requires effort. Ultimately, you must do it for yourself. It takes work and time. And it hurts.

If You Want Something Done, You've Gotta Do It Yourself: Change Takes Responsibility

Right before I sat down to write this page, I saw an infomercial for exercise equipment that exercises for you. The host of the show enthusiastically proclaimed how you could lose weight fast and easy without even breaking a sweat. ("What's so bad about that and where can I get it?" you might ask.)

This message troubles me. It suggests you can change without investing any of your own sweat equity. But change is not a drop-off laundry service where you can get someone else to clean, press, and fix you. You must do the hard work and you must do it yourself.

Before you experience the change you want in your life, you may need to learn how to do something you don't already know how to do. Perhaps you'll need a teacher to explain it or show you how, but you'll ultimately still need to learn and do the work for yourself.

It's like having a personal trainer. What if you don't know how to lift the weights properly to avoid injury? What machines do you use to work your triceps? What if you don't even know where your triceps are? The trainer will explain, demonstrate, and even encourage you, but you will eventually have to lift the weights and do the workout yourself. Unfortunately, the trainer cannot exercise for you. But fortunately, he or she cannot experience the great results of your exercise either...you will! The following story about myself illustrates just how wonderful the results are when you put in the work.

I-Witness Testimony: Pray Peggy Doesn't Drown

A few years ago, I lost my motivation to exercise regularly and noticed I was putting on weight. In order to motivate myself to work out because evidently, looking at myself naked in the mirror wasn't enough, I decided I would compete in a triathlon. The race was a half-mile swim in open water, a twelve-mile bike ride, and a three-mile run.

I had overcome my fear of the big slide at the pool, but I still wasn't a good swimmer. I decided to sign up for a five-week adult swim class at a recreation center near my home. My swim teacher was a sixteen-year-old named Ariel. She was adorable with flawlessly clear skin, perfectly shaped eyebrows, and a tiny diamond stud in the side of her nose.

After the first two weeks of lessons, Ariel apparently didn't have much confidence that I'd be able to build my endurance in enough time to compete in the triathlon. Every week, she would ask me the same two questions. Every week, I'd give her the same two answers.

"When is your triathlon?" she'd ask.

"It's on July 16," I'd answer.

"And how far do you have to swim?" she'd ask.

"I have to swim fifteen laps," I'd answer.

Ariel would respond the same way every time: "I don't know if you'll be ready."

My lessons ended one month before the race. I was beginning to believe that Ariel might be right. I could swim only one lap without stopping.

Whenever people asked how my training was going, I answered, "Pray I don't drown."

On my way to the pool one morning, I decided I would do something different. Instead of continuing to struggle with freestyle, I tried the breaststroke. The change was amazing! I swam every day. By the end of the month, I could do the entire half-mile without stopping.

While I needed lessons and Ariel's assistance to introduce me to proper swimming techniques, I couldn't depend on her to swim for me. I couldn't even depend on her to cheer me on. I had to do the work myself. I also had to make up my mind that I wasn't going to be discouraged and give up because it was hard and someone else didn't believe I could do it.

If I had passively expected Ariel to make me swim, I never would have succeeded. I had to take what Ariel taught me and motivate myself, despite her less than optimistic attitude.

Tick-tock, Tick-tock: Change Takes Time

Learning new skills takes time. I didn't learn to swim overnight. It took weeks of daily workouts to build the endurance to successfully complete my triathlon. Change requires patience.

In this society of microwaves, drive-thru windows, and overnight shipping, it's easy to want fast and easy answers to your daily problems. The culture conditions you to expect quick results. Then it labels you with attention deficit and impulse control disorders when you can't wait.

The key to waiting patiently is to remain focused on your goal while simultaneously and diligently pursuing the small tasks that will move you toward that goal.

I'm reminded of my friend, Leland Melvin, an astronaut who would eventually fly to the International Space Station. Leland's launch was originally scheduled to occur on a Thursday afternoon in December. The morning of the launch, the crew was informed of a problem with the fuel tank sensors, which would delay the launch until Friday. On Friday, the launch was delayed until Saturday.

On Saturday, the launch was delayed until Sunday. On Sunday, the launch was delayed a whole month. Sixty-three days after the original date, the shuttle finally launched.

I asked Leland, "What do you and your crew do while the launch is delayed?"

He replied, "We're still doing sims [simulations] and getting ready."

Rather than wallowing in frustration about the delay, the astronauts occupied themselves with the many essential tasks required to prepare for the launch.

Also consider the farmer who must wait for his crops to grow. He cannot do anything to make his corn grow faster. But, while he is waiting, he is busy plowing the fields, fertilizing the ground, watering the plants, and chasing away the crows. He is busy waiting.

Patience produces perseverance. With perseverance, you will work steadily without giving up. Perseverance produces character. Character enables you to live and celebrate as if you already have everything you need and desire while you remain busy waiting for those things to actually manifest in your life.

When you encounter difficult circumstances, be glad. Consider it an opportunity to practice patient endurance, set new goals, work hard, and watch with confident expectation as your life changes. A long race is not won by merely the fastest runner. It is won by the person who endures until the end.

No Gray Areas: All or Nothing Thinking

Change takes work, responsibility, patience, and perseverance. Even so, when you assume your only choices are the hard thing or the easy thing, your circumstances seem more difficult than they really are. Could there be a middle ground? For example, when your alarm goes off in the morning, waking you so you can go to the gym, is it hard for you to get up? Instead of jumping straight out of bed, do you decide to skip the gym altogether and go back to sleep? But that's not your only option. You could hit snooze a few times and still get up later, going to the gym for at least a little while. Some time at the gym is better than no time. It doesn't have to be all or nothing. Change is hard when you view it as black or white. Why not add a little gray to your view?

Facing Your Failures Hurts: What You've Done and Are Doing Isn't Working

Have you ever invested time and effort into a project and it failed? What do you do when what you are doing isn't working? Staying in a situation when it is going nowhere is not the same as persevering through a process. You've been doing everything you should be doing. For a time, it worked. But, for some reason, what's worked in the past is no longer working now. You might think that sticking it out when things are clearly failing is honorable. Really, it's simply ineffective and leads to suffering.

Have you ever continued doing what you've been doing solely to justify your previous efforts and choices? You might think, "If I stop doing this, I have to admit to myself that what I was doing wasn't working." Ouch, that hurts. Who wants to face the fact that you missed another better opportunity because you were doing something that failed in the end? You start singing the "shoulda-coulda-woulda" blues. Regret is a painful pill to swallow.

Facing Your Shame Hurts: What You've Done and Are Doing is Wrong

What happens when things don't work out because what you are doing is wrong or hurts others? Doing

41

something wrong usually requires that you apologize to someone. Rather than say you are sorry, it's easier to justify your previous actions by continuing to do the same things.

Have you ever done or said something that you thought was funny, but the humor was based on making fun of someone else? A friend confronted me about this once. I felt so painfully ashamed. As it turns out, I was making fun of a group, of which he was a member. Not only did the pain come from offending him, I also realized that what I had said was just simply unkind. I didn't like the feeling of my behavior being inconsistent with who I thought I was.

The good news is that I felt shame, showing myself that this behavior was unacceptable to me. It would be a sign of poor character to defend myself, make excuses, or, even worse, blame him for being too sensitive and continue with my bad behavior.

When you are made aware of something that needs to change, it is often painful. The pain can point you to areas that need your attention. Or the pain can be a powerful reminder to never do it again. But the pain can also become the very reason why you won't change. It hurts to be aware of your shortcomings or acknowledge that what you are doing is wrong. It's less painful to hide from the need to change. You would have to say to yourself, "If I want to change, I first have to admit that what I was doing before was wrong." And that hurts.

Reflection Questions

What have you expected someone else to do for you that you need to do yourself?

What would you start doing if it were easy?

Do Something Different...For a Change

What would you stop doing if it were easy?

What are you too ashamed to admit?

Chapter Three Power Points

- Change requires responsibility.
- Change takes work.
- Change takes time.
- Change hurts.

Chapter Four
Change Comes at a Cost

Have you ever held on to something or someone longer than you should because you didn't want to lose it? Doing something different costs you what you want. But holding on when things aren't right will usually cost you even more. When you change, you lose. But, when you lose, you win. Let me show you what I mean.

Holier Than Thou: Change Sets You Apart

"You used to be fun."

"You're different. What happened to you?"

Have you ever heard statements like these? When you change, you will lose relationships. Once you're different, the people around you can't remain the same and still be in a relationship with you. You no longer have much in common.

As you start to change, friends and family may subtly discourage you from changing. If you give up smoking, stop eating junk food, quit having one-night stands, and stop complaining, the same people who smoke, eat junk food, have one-night stands, and complain can no longer freely do these things around you. When you change, the relationship must change. And that change sometimes means the relationship will end.

With all the great changes you will be making in your life, you'll become increasingly different from the person you were before. People who used to be in relationship with you will say things like, "Ever since you _____ [fill in the blank with whatever changes you've made], now you think you're too good to be around us."

But be encouraged. This is just code for the following, "Ever since you _____, I feel inadequate around you. My behavior seems so inappropriate. But since I'm not as courageous and strong as you, I don't think I'll be able to change like you did. Instead, I'm going to have to put you down to feel better about myself."

Change sets you apart and others may dislike how they feel about themselves around you. This doesn't mean you are better than them or even think you are. It simply means you are different; you are set apart from the crowd. What you lose in company, you gain in the benefits that come from the changes you have made in your life.

One's Company: Change Compels You to Let Go

Certain friends may distance themselves from you, but you may also discover that you need to give up the relationships that you sense are no longer right for you. You might be in a romantic relationship or friendship that you once believed was meeting your needs. But now that you are changing, this may no longer be the case.

You may not want to let go of this relationship because, to some extent, you still believe you are getting what you need and want out of it. But examine the change that is occurring in your life and fully consider what you want in the future. You may be surprised to discover that remaining in the relationship, that is, if it stays the way it currently is, is actually a barrier to you getting what you truly are needing and seeking. The very thing you are holding on to prevents you from getting what you want. Once you realize this, you have the hope of actually getting your heart's desires.

Abandon Ship: The Fear of Losing

People often stay in relationships and circumstances because they are afraid of what they will lose if they let go. Fear can be a huge factor in avoiding loss. When I was an intern at the end of my graduate training in psychology, I worked in the adolescent unit of a psychiatric hospital for several months. My supervisor drew an analogy between addictions and being on a sinking ship. If you keep doing what you're doing and stay where you are, you are definitely going down. You may feel like you're standing on a solid foundation, but the ship is sinking.

He used to say that recovery from an addiction is like stepping onto a lifeboat. If you'll just get off the sinking ship, you have a chance. But, during those seconds when you are stepping from the sinking ship to the lifeboat, there is nothing beneath your feet. You are suspended in air.

He asked the teenage addicts the following question in every group session, "Are you willing to have nothing for as long as it takes to build something healthy in its place?"

A variation on this question is also relevant to your relationships. Are you willing to be alone for as long as it takes to build a healthy relationship? Is your fear of losing preventing you from ultimately gaining?

The funny thing is that it's usually crystal clear when the ship you are on is sinking. People are running around, getting their life vests on. Water is splashing at your feet. Emergency sirens are going off all around you. But you act like you don't hear the commotion. Maybe it's easier to pretend you are not sinking. But you are going down.

The only way to save yourself is to jump off the sinking ship and get onto the lifeboat. But it feels like you have nothing beneath you during the time it takes you to leap over to the lifeboat. Jumping requires you to leave everything you know behind and trust, even when it feels like nothing is there.

I occasionally imagine what would happen if my home caught on fire. I'd want to get out immediately, but I'd want to go back for certain things because I wouldn't want to leave them behind. To lose them is to live; to hold on is certain death.

Perhaps you want to stay on the sinking ship because you fear the feeling of losing everything and having nothing. You would rather have the illusion of something, even if that something is sinking. Ironically, fear keeps you in a place where you are guaranteed to experience disaster. Remember, the ship is sinking. But the captain doesn't really always have to go down with the ship.

I Give Up: Sometimes You're Gonna Lose

Change is a stripping process. It costs you parts of yourself. It transforms who you are, what you do, and what you enjoy. Have you ever seen a piece of fine antique furniture that's been refinished? Someone had a keen enough eye to recognize that beneath the peeling, chipping, and worn-out finish was a solid piece of wood with a pleasing design. It just needed a little work. Okay, it will take a lot of hard work. Stripping can be a painful, arduous process.

Loss of Your Identity: Losing Who You Are

One of my favorite movies is *Terms of Endearment* starring Shirley MacLaine and Debra Winger. Debra Winger's character, Emma, is married to Flap, a mediocre English professor. Emma suspects Flap is cheating on her, but he never openly admits it. When Emma is dying of cancer, Flap faces the prospect of losing the wife he's taken for granted. In a rare moment of sincerity, Flap says to Emma, "I'm thinking about my identity, and not having one anymore. I mean, who am I if I'm not the man who's failing Emma?"[3]

That question is at the heart of this book. Who would you be if you did something different? Who are you if you

---

[3] *Terms of Endearment* (Paramount Pictures, 1983)

are not overweight? Who are you if you are not a victim? Who are you if you are not a successful CEO?

When describing yourself to others, do you say, "I'm the type of person who…"? When others appropriately confront you about your behavior and the need to change, do you tell them that this is just who you are and they can either love you or leave you? Are you the type of person who stays the same and lives your label? Or are you an individual who is unique, who can change, and who is growing? Living your label is an easy out. It's nothing more than an excuse to stay the same and avoid the work, fear, and cost of change.

When you decide to do something different for a change, it provides you with an opportunity to redefine who you are. Who are you if you are not the person "who is failing Emma"? You are the man who is working hard to be someone new. You are the woman who is developing her character by taking a risk. When you change, you lose who you were, but you gain a whole new you, the real you! When you let go of your old identity, you are brand new, and the old things pass away.

I Want My Blankey: Losing Your Comfort

What will you do if you don't do what you've always done? In addition to losing your identity, you lose your comfort zone when you change. What you are used to doing gives you a clearly delineated list of responsibilities and tasks. It feels safer to follow this list and execute the same patterns of behavior that you're used to than to do something different.

I know a woman who continues to put up with inappropriate, destructive behavior from her daughter. If she did something different, she wouldn't have much else to focus on. Innovation takes effort, creativity, and courage. Giving up old patterns and focusing your attention elsewhere is like quitting your job. Repeating ineffective behaviors gives you job security.

When you do something different, you trade what you know for something unknown. You lose who you are, what you do, and the comfort that such consistency and predictability provide.

Have you ever been fired or laid off and catapulted completely out of your comfort zone, but found yourself a year later in a completely better position? That's what happened to Irene.

I-Witness Testimony: Irene Goes Fishing

Some time ago, a boyfriend and I moved to a new city to get a fresh start in life. We were both ready for something different, and we were excited about the possibilities of what was ahead for us, individually and with each other. Moving from my hometown was a huge step as I was quite comfortable where I was. But something inside of me said it was time to go.

I'm reminded of a sermon I once heard where Jesus tells his disciples to cast their nets into deeper waters in order to get an abundant harvest. For me, this meant I needed to get out of the familiar "shallow waters" to which I had grown accustomed. I'm not suggesting that everyone must leave their homes in order to grow, but this is what I needed to do.

Several years after moving, a number of dramatic incidents occurred in my life. My boyfriend and I broke up. My mother died unexpectedly. I was laid off.

I had no idea what I was going to do. I had bills to pay. I started feeling a bit sorry for myself. As a single woman, I did not have another source of income. One month grew into three. Three months became six. Six months became ten. All told, I was unemployed for one year.

Throughout these hard times, I needed to get over one thing: the need to know before taking a step. My fear often got in the way of doing what I needed to do.

51

I eventually overcame my fear of the unknown. During my time off, I thought of a business I'd love to start. I sold my home. Now, all that I gave up has been restored, and I've gained even more.

I've learned I can stay in a familiar place where I know what will happen day in and day out and live a partially fulfilling life. Or I can cast my net into the deep, unfamiliar places where my abundant harvest awaits. I think I'll go fishing.

Losing your comfort often moves you to redefine what's important or do what you really want to do. Irene took a risk, sold her home, and started planning a new business. It all may feel like a crisis as it is happening. But, when you get through the process and look back to where you were and where you are now, I know, like Irene, you'll say it was all worth it.

Loss of Your Control: Losing It All

If you are like most people, you do not like feeling out of control. Being out of control means you no longer have the power to influence or direct your behavior, emotions, or situations. And that does not feel good at all.

As a therapist, I occasionally used clinical hypnosis with my clients, especially those with anxiety issues. Think of a hypnotic trance as a deliberately induced state of deep relaxation. There's nothing spooky or mystical about it. You'd be surprised, though, how many people didn't want to learn hypnosis because they feared losing control. They were concerned I would make them do things they didn't want to do or they would go into a trance and never come out. Because it was new and unfamiliar, they hadn't yet learned that I couldn't make them do anything they didn't want to do.

When you do something different, you may not initially feel like you are in control of your own behavior and emotions or situations you find yourself in. But, over time, this sense of being out of control will diminish.

In the meantime, I'd like to persuade you that you don't have as much control over other people and situations as you may like to think in the first place. Yes, you can have control over your own behavior and emotions. But you must let go of your attachment to the idea that you are, could be, or even should be in control of everyone and everything around you.

You may think I am exaggerating to say this. But think about the last several times you have suffered or even been disappointed, angry, or frustrated. You likely expected people to act the way you wanted them to, or you expected things to turn out the way you desired. And you likely believed that you could control or should be able to control those people and situations. Otherwise, you would not have felt disappointment, anger, or frustration to the degree you did.

This perception or illusion of control is something you will gladly give up when you realize it is a barrier to the change you desire. It takes a great deal of energy to try to be in control of all the things in your environment. You are still absolutely responsible for yourself, but you are not responsible for everything that happens around you. It is liberating when you accept that other people's actions are their own. It frees you to focus on your own thoughts, emotions, reactions, and behaviors. Once you experience this freedom, you will be committed to a lifestyle that is more focused on introspection—that is, attending to and examining your own motives, thoughts, and feelings rather than those of others.

Reflection Questions

Which of your relationships keep you from changing?

Which of your relationships inspire you to change?

Are you willing to have nothing while you build something healthy in its place?

What would you do if you had nothing left to lose?

Chapter Four Power Points

- Change will cost you relationships.
- Change will cost you your identity and security.
- Change will cost you your comfort.
- Change will cost you control.

PART TWO

Chapter Five
What Your Therapist Knows

Psychologists measure intelligence by reporting your intelligence quotient (IQ). Historically, IQ was calculated by comparing your mental age to your chronological age. When your mental age is greater than your chronological age, you have a high IQ.

There are many ways to maintain your mental acumen or intellectual functioning as you age. Expose yourself regularly to intellectual stimulation. Drive home a new way each day. Keep your mind mentally active by reading and doing crossword puzzles. In other words, always do something different.

I'd like to suggest that you work on also increasing what I call your change quotient (CQ). Think of your CQ as your openness to change relative to your willingness to change. Openness to change is the degree to which you want to have change in your life or experience life differently. Willingness to change is the degree to which you will do whatever is required to experience that change.

When both your openness and willingness are equally high, you have a high CQ. In other words, you want change, and you will do whatever it takes to achieve it. When either your openness or willingness is low, your CQ will be low. You are not likely to experience change.

Ask yourself these questions:

- Do I want next year to be different than this one?
- Am I interested in being somewhere other than where I am right now?
- Do I have goals for myself and my future?
- Do I really want change in at least one important area of my life?

59

If you answered yes, then you have a high openness to change. If you answered no, it's probably because of the reasons discussed in the first part of this book. Change is hard. It's scary, and it comes at a cost.

Next, ask yourself these questions:

- Am I willing to do whatever it takes to get to where I want to go?
- Have I made a plan for how to get there?
- Do I keep trying even after I fail?
- Do I actively seek out information when I am not sure what to do?

If you answered yes, then you have a high willingness to change. If you answered no, you are probably like most people. You don't really want to change. But the purpose of this book is to show you the reasons why and persuade you to change your mind.

I don't know that I can say that one is more significant than the other. Both openness and willingness are critical to doing something different. They ideally should be in balance, where desire is matched with equal initiative. The good news is that you can enhance your overall CQ by understanding and applying the principles discussed in this book. Your therapist also has valuable information that will help you to experience lasting change in your life.

Just Give Me Three Weeks: What Your Therapist Knows about Change

Have you ever made a New Year's resolution? Have you ever planned to quit smoking, eat healthier, lose weight, or gossip less? Psychologists believe that if you do something for twenty-one days, it will become a habit. For example, if you would commit to exercising every day for three weeks, it would become a part of your routine and something you might even look forward to doing.

Making a habit of exercising is hard enough, but what about making a habit of holding your tongue? Have you ever told yourself to get rid of anger, bitterness, and harsh words? It lasts for a short time, maybe an hour or maybe a day or two. Then you just forget. This book will show you exactly what you need to do to experience lasting change.

What does your therapist know about how change occurs? Drs. James Prochaska, John Norcross, and Carlo DiClemente have developed one of the most widely studied theories of change. Their Transtheoretical Model of Change[4] centers around five stages that you must go through in order to experience change: precontemplation, contemplation, preparation, action, and maintenance.

According to Prochaska, Norcross, and Diclimente, in the precontemplation stage, you are not thinking about or interested in changing. In the contemplation stage, you are thinking about changing and evaluating the pros and cons, but you have not yet taken any steps. In the preparation stage, you begin to develop a plan of what you will do to achieve your desired goals. In the action stage, you are actually taking steps to change. And, finally, in the maintenance stage, you take action only as needed to prevent slipping back or having a relapse.

Prochaska, Norcross, and DiClemente have applied their stages of change to behaviors such as smoking, overeating, drinking, and drug addiction. They have concluded that interventions should be matched to the stage you are in. For example, you would never use a free sample of a nicotine patch that you got in the mail (action) if you are not interested in quitting smoking to begin with

---

[4] J.O. Prochaska, J.C. Norcross, and C.C. DiClemente, *Changing for Good: The Revolutionary Program that Explains the Six Stages of Change and Teaches You How to Free Yourself From Bad Habits* (New York: W. Morrow, 1994).

(precontemplation). This is consistent with your CQ. Your openness to change, which is akin to the contemplation stage, must be equally matched by your willingness to change (preparation and action) before you will experience change in your life.

If you are reading this book, you are at least in the contemplation stage. The first part of this book is designed to help you move to the preparation stage. And the third part of this book will show you what steps to take to achieve the change you want in your life. Remember, you cannot keep doing things the same way and have anything change. You cannot have something different if you fail to do something different. Perhaps you've heard insanity defined as doing the same things over and over, yet expecting different results.

Am I Really Nuts? What Your Therapist Knows about Mental Illness

According to the National Institute of Mental Health, about one in four American adults is mentally ill and has some diagnosable mental disorder.[5] Check three friends. If they seem okay, then it must be you! That's an old joke that reflects a serious statistic.

What is a mental disorder? Psychiatrists and psychologists define a mental disorder as a pattern of thinking, feeling, and behaving that causes significant distress or dysfunction.[6] In other words, how you tend to think about the world makes you feel so bad that you can't do the

---

[5] National Institute of Mental Health, *The Numbers Count: Mental Disorders in America*, 2008, www.nimh.nih.gov/health/publications/the-numbers-count-mental-disorders-in-america.shtml.

[6] American Psychiatric Association, *Diagnostic and Statistical Manual of Mental Disorders, Fourth edition, Text Revision* (Washington, DC: American Psychiatric Association, 2000).

things you need to do. Frequent crying, dramatic mood swings, hallucinations, and compulsive rituals are symptoms of some of the more common mental disorders.

Four of the ten leading causes of disability in the United States are mental disorders, including major depression, bipolar disorder, schizophrenia, and obsessive-compulsive disorder. With one in four people diagnosed with a mental disorder, you shouldn't be surprised to learn that the Surgeon General's 1999 report on mental health stated that 15 percent of the American adult population uses mental health services, including psychotherapy, in any given year.[7]

Psychotherapy can be simply defined as using psychological techniques and a special relationship with a trained professional to produce emotional, cognitive, and behavioral change. There are many types of talk therapy, but no evidence suggests that any one type is superior to the others.

Psychologists believe that the key elements to any successful psychotherapy are a new perspective or rationale for your problems, an empathic, trusting, caring relationship, and hope. Gaining a new perspective is an important part of why people benefit from therapy, when they benefit at all.

The surgeon general also concluded that most people with a diagnosable mental disorder do not receive the psychotherapy they justifiably need, but some of the people who are in psychotherapy do not have a diagnosable mental disorder. Unfortunately, many of the people who truly need mental health intervention are not getting it.

---

[7] U.S. Department of Health and Human Services, *Mental Health: A Report of the Surgeon General* (Rockville, Md.: U.S. Department of Health and Human Services, Substance Abuse and Mental Health Services Administration, Center for Mental Health Services, National Institutes of Health, National Institute of Mental Health, 1999).

While research shows it is possible to change without psychotherapy, *please consult a mental health professional if you think you may have a serious mental illness.*

Whether or not you've been diagnosed with a mental disorder or you've been in therapy, you will always benefit from having a new perspective and doing something different. Psychotherapy has helped many people, but there are also people who don't really need therapy and people who are in therapy who never change.

Why then are so many ordinary people in psychotherapy? Why do so many people in therapy never change? Most likely, your therapist knows, but he or she may not tell you. Continue reading, and I will tell you in the next chapter.

Reflection Questions

What have you learned in therapy that helped you change?

What are you still doing despite your therapy?

Chapter Five Power Points

- Know your change quotient (CQ).
- It takes twenty-one days to form a new habit.
- Therapy works when it gives you a new perspective.
- Consult a mental health professional if you think you may have a serious mental illness.

Chapter Six
What Your Therapist May Not Tell You

You and your therapist are dancing two sides of the same dance. You don't really want to change and your therapist may not encourage or require you to change.

Regardless of what you are doing or how you are living, your therapist is trained to accept you without judgment. Usually, however, the only result of this "unconditional positive regard" is that you feel better about not doing better.

During the course of therapy, your therapist may help you to create the illusion that you are doing something constructive and meaningful. This happens even if change never occurs. Many therapists implicitly give you permission to continue doing the same things without changing. Why would your therapist do this?

I may be branded a therapeutic heretic for saying this, but your therapist would be out of business if he or she confronted this illusion and made returning to therapy contingent upon you actually doing something different and, in most cases, doing what you already know you should. The longer you remain in therapy, the more money your therapist makes. This may not be a totally conscious motivation, but it is a conflict of interest nonetheless.

When therapy does not directly challenge your thinking and behavior, it inhibits you from doing something truly different. Some types of therapy, more than others, allow you to remain passive. You should avoid therapy that is an extension of the same patterns of thinking and behavior that got you stuck to begin with. But your therapist may not tell you this.

And ... Cut! Reading from Your Script

Have you ever gone through a difficult situation and shared the story with a friend in great detail but then realized halfway through that you've already told them the same story practically verbatim? I call this "reading from your script."

Within limits, the telling of your story is valuable to you and your therapist. Most noteworthy, it allows you to see the significant issues and impact of your past on your current problems. But, as long as you are telling and retelling your story, you are focused on the past. Reading from your script distracts you from focusing on solutions and change in the present. You already know how the story is going to end. There are no surprises. In that way, reading from your script can give you a sense of security. But it won't give you the change you want.

But, Anyway, Like I Was Saying

As a therapist, I might interject a question or make some profound statement. After a momentary pause, the client would usually respond, "Well, yeah. But, anyway, like I was saying..." He or she would continue with his or her story, as if I had never spoken or I weren't even there. This happens outside of therapy in real life, too.

Have you ever suspected someone knew what was wrong in his life and, more importantly, knew how to fix it? You can ask him, but you should not tell him that you're talking about him. Just say it's about a friend of yours.

You could say, "Joe, you remember Susie, don't you? Well, Susie has been in this relationship for years that is going nowhere."

Inevitably, Joe will respond with several suggestions of what Susie should do differently. Joe will have all kinds of insights into how Susie came to be the way she is, how she could improve herself, and what she should do next.

But an amazing thing happens when you ask Joe what stops him from ending or fixing the bad relationship he's been in for years. Suddenly, Joe doesn't have any insights. He doesn't know why he's stuck. He rambles on, reading his script about how bad his situation is. As soon as you reflect back to him what you just heard him say, he will make excuses for why he remains in a relationship that he just described a minute ago as being unbearable. He rationalizes and justifies it, but he complains about it at the same time.

Well, friend, I know someone who is just like Joe. You!

I once worked with Staci, a bright, ambitious college student. She came in for a session one day and matter-of-factly announced she was dating a married man. Implicitly seeking my approval for what she was doing, she gave me a list of reasons why having sex with this married man and being emotionally invested in him was a reasonable thing to have started and continue.

Believing that what she was doing was wrong and suspecting she knew that what she was doing was wrong, I patiently listened to her read from her script. Unable to confront her directly because I was trained to leave my personal values out of therapy, I asked her the following simple question, "If this were your little sister telling you what you just told me, what would you say to her?"

Without hesitation, she responded, "I would tell her to stop seeing him because it is wrong to date a married man. I could never condone such a thing for her."

"Why then," I innocently inquired, "is it wrong for her but okay for you?"

Staci paused for two or three seconds and then proceeded to read from her script again, as if the preceding dialogue had never taken place.

Have you ever continued to explain and rationalize your point of view, reading from your script, until your therapist or friend said what you wanted to hear rather than what you needed to hear? You want to hear that what you're doing is okay or you're doing the best you can under the circumstances. You might even want to hear your therapist or friend admit that he or she would do the same thing.

By the way, be careful of listening to advice from people who are in the same predicament as you. People sometimes will encourage you to continue doing what you're doing simply because it justifies the very (often wrong) thing they are doing themselves.

I've Been Seeing My Therapist for Years: What Your Therapist May Not Tell You about Why You Keep Coming Back

Early in my career as a therapist, I observed that many of my clients never seemed to get better. Thankfully, I had a small group of clients who readily set therapeutic goals and took concrete steps, with my guidance, to achieve those goals. One of their most important goals was to eventually get out of therapy.

Then I had another group of clients. I listened to these same people complain, week after week, about the same things, relationships, and situations. They stayed in the exact same place or even got worse! But, for some reason, they kept coming back.

This was a curious observation. Why would someone who is not being helped keep coming back for more? Would you go back to the same mechanic if your car kept stalling after several consecutive visits to the auto shop? Would you continue going to the same restaurant if the waiter never got your order right and the food always tasted awful? But this is what people do in therapy.

Your therapist won't tell you that one way they keep you coming back is by labeling or pathologizing your behavior. If you are diagnosed with a label, you need expert assistance to change. You convince yourself that you don't know what to do about a situation or you don't have the resources to change it.

You believe your therapist has special powers or knowledge that will transform you. You keep coming back because you believe your therapist knows something you don't know and can do something you can't do yourself. Just for a moment, pretend you did know how. Then what would stop you?

In reality, you already have the power and know everything you need to live a fulfilled life, but you choose to stay stuck. There is a payoff for remaining where you are and remaining in therapy. Think for a moment about what that might be for you. You already know what you need to do, but there are benefits for not doing it.

You Can Run and You Can Hide

Remaining in therapy and not changing gives you a place to hide. You can avoid the discomfort you experience as a result of already knowing what you should be doing differently. You can bury your head in the proverbial sands of therapy, postponing the need to do what you know to be right, effective, or healthy. It is your "get out of life free" card.

Entering and remaining in therapy gets you off the hook, buys you time, and relieves you of your own personal responsibility for change. Even though the car isn't getting fixed, taking it back week after week spares you the difficulty and responsibility of having to figure out what's wrong and fix it yourself. It doesn't work, but, if nothing else, you don't have to feel guilty about not at least trying to get it fixed.

71

Therapy makes you feel less uncomfortable about the way your life is heading. After all, you can tell people, "I'm in therapy, you know." Being in therapy makes you feel better about not taking the necessary steps to actually get better. And the real shame is that the therapist is a willing participant in this game of "hide-and-no-seek."

Reflection Questions

What is the payoff for what you are or are not doing?

What is the payoff for remaining in therapy?

What would happen if you gave up those benefits?

Chapter Six Power Points

- How you do life is how you do therapy.
- You already have the power and know everything you need to live a fulfilled life, but you choose to stay stuck.
- Therapy gives you a place to hide.

Chapter Seven
In a Rut

Just like you do in other areas of your life, you might also find yourself getting stuck in therapy. These ruts can become barriers to change, both in and out of therapy.

Feelings, Nothing More Than Feelings

It is common practice for your therapist to encourage you to focus on your feelings. Feelings are like Geiger counters or the metal detectors that beachcombers use to find lost items. Where you have strong, negative feelings, you will find something significant going on below the surface. But merely talking only about feelings prevents you from doing something different.

You want to be careful that you don't start to worship at the altar of your feelings. It is easy to let your feelings define you rather than simply describe how you are at the moment.

In the Spanish language, you say, "Tengo fear" or "I have fear." In English, you say, "I am afraid." The verb "to be" or "am" is equivalent to an equal sign. I equal fear. The Spanish expression, "I have fear," conveys a temporary state. Feelings are something you can have now and not have later. If I am fear, I will always be fear! This is subtle but significant. Your mind literally interprets feelings in a cause and effect fashion. If you believe something is disappointing, unfair, or regrettable, you will feel sad, even if what you believe is not objectively true. We'll explore this further in chapter ten.

Too Focused on Others: Anger, Judgment, and Blame

Have you ever been so angry with someone else that you didn't see the role you played in the incident? Are you so judgmental of others that you fail to see how bad your own behavior is? Have you ever blamed someone for doing something wrong but later realized that you were just as much (if not more) at fault?

Therapists who do couples counseling encounter the blame game all the time. Your partner criticizes you. Rather than considering the possibility that he or she could be right, you immediately point the finger back at him or her. You identify something that he or she has done that is similar. It might not even be similar, but it's something that bugs you, too. In turn, your partner is now on the defensive. The next thing you know, you are arguing about what he or she does! Pretty clever, huh? In fact, it's masterful if you really never want to change.

Anger is another culprit. It plays a role in the fight-or-flight response. It gives you the motivation needed to survive a perceived threat or danger. Anger is a good thing under the right circumstances. Righteous anger or indignation is an appropriate response to something that is unfair or mean.

But beware of what your therapist might call "catharsis," that is, the venting or release of your anger to gain relief from it. For some people, catharsis can actually feed anger rather than relieve it. Not only is prolonged anger bad for your health, it also keeps you from changing.

As long as you are focused on what you perceive someone else has done to you, whether it was fair or not, you are not focused on what you can do to change. Anger, along with judgment and blame toward others, are smoke screens that obscure your own faults. When you focus your feelings primarily on others, you don't have to examine your own behavior. Don't let your therapist keep you stuck in this rut. Remember, the only person you can change is you!

Also, when you're focused on anger, you are choosing to be disconnected. It is impossible to get close to someone you are angry with. This applies even to yourself! If you want to connect with others and yourself in a genuine and intimate way, you must be willing to let go of anger and forgive.

Too Focused on the Future: Worry

Do you spend a lot of time in therapy worrying? How often does your therapist remind you that you have no control over others and you have little control over the future? Your actions today influence the outcomes you experience tomorrow, but you cannot literally change tomorrow. Worry is an agonizing emotion that results from believing you can know and change the future. Have you ever found yourself thinking, "I just know it's going to turn out bad" or "I'm scared he's mad at me; I'm afraid about what he might do"? The act of worrying is an unconscious attempt to change reality. It's as if you are saying to yourself, "If I worry about it enough, it will change."

Worrying never changed anything. Well, that's not exactly true. Worrying can change something pleasant into something miserable. I learned this lesson the hard way on my honeymoon.

I-Witness Testimony: Peggy the Worrywart

On our way to Florida to catch a honeymoon cruise to the Bahamas, our car broke down. After calling for a tow truck and getting the car to an auto shop, it was evening when the mechanic finally gave us the news. They would need to keep the car for several days to order parts and make the necessary repairs. Our cruise was departing early the next morning. We were still more than four hundred miles away. Minutes before the nearest car rental company closed, we were able to get a car. We got to Florida just in the nick of time.

The problem was resolved. We would just pick up the car when we returned from our cruise, right? Wrong! I worried the entire time. Sitting on the peaceful beach with my new husband, a jumble of thoughts raced through my head.

"What if nothing serious was really wrong and they are just taking advantage of us because we are from out of state?"

"What if they charge us thousands of dollars to fix the car?"

"What if the car is not ready when we return?"

"What if they can't fix it at all and we have to buy a new car to get back home?"

"What if I just slit my throat and die right here right now?" my new husband must have been thinking.

Thankfully, he didn't slit his throat. Instead, he said, "Worrying won't change anything. It won't make the car cost less or be ready any faster. So you might as well just stop thinking about it. Let's enjoy ourselves."

Wow! What a revelation! I wasn't even consciously aware of what I had been doing. It was difficult and took a lot of effort, but I was determined to not let worry ruin our honeymoon. I let go of any remaining thoughts about the future of the car and instead focused on the here and now.

Worrying may come naturally to you, but do you like how it feels? Does it produce the results you want? Do you worry about your finances or health, but never change your behavior? Worrying will never add a single hour to your life. Stop worrying. Instead, do something different!

Too Focused on Yourself: Just Beat It

So now you're mad at yourself for worrying too much. When you realize your behavior is inappropriate or unacceptable by your own standards, are you unforgiving and hard on yourself? You can focus too much blame on others, and you can also focus too much blame on yourself.

When you spend a lot of time beating yourself up for your mistakes, you are not spending much time changing the behavior that led to those mistakes. Be careful not to hide behind guilt or shame. Don't use them as excuses not to change.

Shame is the painful and regrettable conscious realization that your behavior was unacceptable. As you read in chapter three, a healthy dose of shame should motivate you to examine your heart and your intentions and cause you to behave differently in the future. But shame can also condemn and paralyze. Some psychologists call this "toxic shame."

Similarly, guilt is a feeling of having done something wrong. Like shame, guilt can motivate you to take responsibility to fix the wrong. But it is easy to allow guilt to relieve you of your responsibility. You might say, "Oh, I feel so guilty for lying and taking that stuff from work." Tomorrow, do you actually stop lying or stealing? Once you let go of guilt and shame, you have only two options:

- Guiltlessly and shamelessly continue your bad behavior. (Psychologists call people like this psychopaths.)
- Don't feel guilty at all because you are doing something different.

As hard as it is to do what is right and as painful as it feels when you do wrong, what you've done or not done is not who you are. Yes, the consequences of what you've done remain. But your past choices are who you were. Who you are can be redefined in every moment as you make new choices and experience new consequences.

Are you willing to turn from your old behavior, forgive yourself for your past mistakes, and put on your new nature? You might think you've made too many mistakes to start over. You may have given up all hope. Well, I'm here to tell you that you can start over. We'll tackle this in the third part of this book.

Reflection Questions

What are you angry about?

What do you worry about?

What do you need to forgive yourself for?

Chapter Seven Power Points

- Don't worship at the altar of feelings.
- Anger distracts and disconnects.
- Worrying never changed anything.
- Beating yourself up keeps you from changing.

Chapter Eight
Why Change?

How do you get motivated to actually want to change? You have to get to the point where you are more afraid to stay where you are than you are to change. When you are finally sick and tired of being sick and tired, then you will really want to change. It just may take a while to get to that point.

Maybe you have been in a twelve-step program like Alcoholics Anonymous (AA). People in AA understand that sometimes it takes hitting rock bottom to be motivated to change. As a therapist, I always tried to help my clients "raise the bottom" and get motivated without having to fall all the way down. Perhaps you have not yet hit rock bottom. I'd like to persuade you that you've already fallen far enough and you don't need to fall any further. Get sick and tired right where you are. Spare yourself the pain of hitting the bottom. Do you want to change? Then pick yourself up, get out of BED, and walk!

Sick and Tired Enough

Even when you are sick and tired, you still may stay stuck because you are not sick and tired enough. Becoming sick and tired enough requires you to carefully assess if you are receiving any hidden rewards for not changing. As you saw in chapter six, there might be some subtle payoff for doing what you've been doing. Search your heart and discover what's keeping you stuck and why you haven't changed yet. Unless you uncover the hidden payoff, you will never be sick and tired enough!

What would it take to make you sick and tired enough? Would realizing that you are actually choosing the very things that are causing your suffering do it? Let me use an example to explain what I mean.

Janet is desperately afraid of being alone, but she married a man whose job keeps him away several months at a time. Because he is gone so often, she feels lonely. Without considering the consequences, she chose to have an affair. This other man comes over when he wants to have sex, but he is otherwise unavailable to her. He spends very little time talking to her and never takes her out. When she is with him, she feels good for the moment. But, as soon as he leaves, she feels ashamed, abandoned, and alone again.

Whenever her husband returns home, she remains emotionally distant because of her guilt and shame. Even when her husband is there, Janet still feels alone and disconnected. She recently discovered her lover has given her a sexually transmitted disease. How can she explain this to her husband? If her husband finds out and her lover leaves her, guess what? The very thing she was afraid of happening will come about. She will be alone. She will have no one to blame but herself. Do you see how Janet's choices bring her the very consequences she so desperately wants to avoid?

Being sick and tired enough starts with making the connection between your own choices and their outcomes. Yes, many things—over which you've had no control— have happened to you. That's what being in BED is all about. But you do have complete control over your responses. Even in the midst of unfortunate circumstances, you have a choice about how you respond. I'll elaborate on this in chapter eleven.

Something's Gotta Give

What are you choosing to make you so sick and tired in the first place? Think of a current situation that you're tired of. Perhaps you are in a relationship that keeps going around and around without moving forward. You've said to yourself or the other person, "I'm sick of this." Nevertheless, you continue on. What have you done to exacerbate the problem? What haven't you done to correct it? Until you carefully examine your patterns and dynamics in this interaction, you will miss your role in maintaining the status quo.

Being sick and tired enough can be the force that makes change happen more quickly. It can open your eyes and allow you to see your situation clearly. You will finally be motivated to permanently change. You know you've been there a thousand times. It's never any different. You're sick of it; you finally see the role you, your thoughts, words, actions, and habits have been playing in the scenario. You may have no control over the other person or situation, but you know you have control over you. You have to decide you're done, turn from what you've been doing, forgive yourself, and move on. It's going to be hard. You know you're scared. It comes at a cost, but you can do it.

Consider Lorraine, a hip, single mother. I had breakfast with her just recently. As she was recounting a few of the things she went through as a child, all I could say was, "Wow!"

She responded, "You don't even know the half of it."

I-Witness Testimony: The Other Half for Lorraine

My mom is addicted to heroin. I'm not sure where my father is. I've been on my own since I was thirteen. I dropped out of high school. I now have two young children by two different men. One of the fathers is involved, but the other is not.

I hate to admit it, but I smoke marijuana every day to deal with all the stress I'm under. Not too long ago, I lost my job. I didn't have any money for food. I receive some public assistance, however, because of the rules, I have to lie about the little bit of money I am making. After some time, I eventually got a temp job, but then my car broke down. I had no way to get to work. I was eventually able to buy a used car, but they are charging me 20 percent interest because my credit is so bad.

My mom is still on drugs; my brother is in prison. When every-thing starts going wrong for them and my sister, they call me. I feel helpless and overwhelmed with the burden to rescue them all.

But look at Lorraine today. Despite her continued drug use, she just completed ninety days on her new permanent job. She is off probation. She's in a beautiful home (Section 8), and she is compassionate to others in need. Lorraine got to the point where she didn't want to continue living the way she was living. She wanted to make different choices.

Every day, she experiences pressure from family members to remain the same. They criticize her and put her down for pulling herself out of the life they are still living. But, once she saw clearly how her own choices brought on much of her heartache, she was finally sick and tired enough! Like Lorraine, when you are finally sick and tired enough, you will also do something different for a change.

Do the Right Thing

Have you ever done something you are not proud of? Would you be pleased to find your secrets posted on the Internet? You pay a high price when you don't do what is right.

In talking with Lorraine and trying to help motivate her to stop smoking marijuana, I framed it as an issue of doing what is right. In addition to the health risks of drug addiction, I wanted her to clearly see the bigger picture. Smoking marijuana is illegal. She could stop smoking marijuana for any number of reasons, so why not stop simply because it is the right thing to do?

Doing wrong things puts you at risk for so many conse-quences. Take the example of Janet, who was cheating on her husband. I'm sure you can agree that, in addition to being wrong, infidelity in marriage also poses many risks. Staying faithful keeps you safe. It protects you from sexually transmitted diseases, the possibly violent actions of a jealous spouse, and the social stigma of being a cheater.

What about smoking marijuana? Lorraine could be arrested for buying marijuana, being under the influence of it, or possessing it. She could go to prison. She could lose her kids and her job. Doing what's right maintains the security of your family and home. Simply put, doing what is right keeps you safe.

When you see yourself doing things that aren't right, it causes you to lose respect for yourself. When others see you doing things that aren't right, it causes them to lose respect for you as well. Lorraine can hold her head up high as she conquers her dependence on marijuana. She can be proud of the example she is setting for her children. How can she possibly command any authority with her kids when she tells them to "just say no" if she is not doing the right thing herself?

Some people are so hardened by their wrong actions that they've lost all remorse. They fail to see themselves as they truly are. Choosing not to change is often due to the pain of seeing yourself for who you really are. But doing what is right will allow you to look yourself in the eye and feel proud of who you are becoming. You may not be there yet, but you can respect the effort and integrity that goes into doing the right thing.

Doing what is right, especially when it is difficult, brings life. You can pat yourself on the back for making the choice to do the right thing in the face of difficult circumstances. It may be a sacrifice to do the hard, but right, thing, but there are always long-term consequences for doing the wrong thing.

Think of the people around you for whom you feel deep respect and admiration. Examine their lives and choices carefully. Why do you admire them? Do you revere certain accomplishments or attributes? Have they overcome hardships? Are they living virtuous lives? When you do what's right, the people around you will honor you, too.

There's Hope in Them Thar Hills!

Are you heartsick? What dreams and goals have you given up on? In what areas of your life do you feel defeated? What are you hopeless about? Well, be encouraged. Change will renew your hope! Seeing yourself in the process of doing something you never thought you'd do heals your heart and brings great joy. Doing something different gives you a feeling of expectation and the belief that good things can happen. It energizes you and gives you the courage to endure.

When something is not changing, it is not living. Stagnant water does not produce life. Doctors are concerned when a baby has not gained enough weight. As long as you live, you change. As long as you change, you live. You are not living to your full potential or being your true self when you are not changing. And when you remain the same and don't change, a part of you dies.

How does change cause you to live? Becoming the real you is the only way to have an authentic connection with yourself and others. An authentic connection is trustworthy, honest, accurate, and true. When you interact with others in an authentic way, you are truly alive. Tanya learned this valuable lesson.

I-Witness Testimony: The Real Tanya Stands Up

At the beginning of a new relationship, I found myself occasionally presenting a slightly altered version of the real me. I realize now that I was trying to make myself more appealing to him. I might say something that I thought would sound good, but it wasn't what I truly believed. It was never too far from the truth, but, nonetheless, it was not my true beliefs.

I also became especially sensitive to what I interpreted as criticism from him. As a result, I began feeling even more inadequate. I tried to avoid rejection by anticipating what I thought he would like rather than just being myself. It was subtle. Probably no one else would ever have noticed. But I knew. I wanted to be accepted for who I was, but I was too afraid to present the bona fide me. How ironic.

I falsely believed that being the real me might cost me something, so I covered her up and altered her in small, seemingly insignificant ways every now and then. What could it possibly cost to be real? I thought it would cost me validation and acceptance. This was an opportunity for me to be viewed as worthwhile and desirable and get over the rejection and failure I had felt in the past.

I eventually realized that not being real and authentic would cost me even more. It would cost me Me! Once I identified this pattern, I stopped pretending and brought out the real me. This was a risk. I might not be accepted. But, regardless of the outcome, I felt energized and free. I found myself before I totally disappeared.

Tanya realized she didn't need to cover up the things she didn't like about herself and she could accept herself for who she was. Her flaws may be difficult and scary to face. Facing them might cost her something, but she learned she couldn't afford to cover them up. When you cover up your flaws, a part of you most certainly dies.

Take a stand for what's important to you. Let the real you be revealed and take root in your convictions. Resist the tendency to let your perceptions of what others think of you alienate you from yourself. You naturally have a desire to pursue and nurture your deepest beliefs and values without fear of rejection. And when you do that, the real you lives!

Why Change? To Do What Works

Not only is change good because it is the right thing to do and it helps you truly live. Change is good because it actually works! Doing the same thing repeatedly with poor results is frustrating and ineffective. It simply does not work. Don't you want to do what actually works?

You wouldn't be reading this book if what you've been doing was working. And doing what you want to do doesn't always lead to the things you want to have. In order to avoid suffering, you must fix what really needs fixing. Take a closer look at Janet. Her choices and actions led to the very thing she didn't want, loneliness.

Consider the alternative. Janet chooses to marry a man who values intimacy and shared activities. She chooses to remain faithful when she feels the temptation to pull away. These choices naturally bring her closer to what she wants most, intimate companionship.

What about Lorraine? She was smoking marijuana to cope with her stress. In her words, it helped her to focus. Focus on what? She had the munchies all the time, and she had gained twenty pounds. When she was high, she wasn't focused on her kids, work, or becoming a better person. Using marijuana to cope with her stress was actually causing her more problems and more stress.

But what if Lorraine chooses to face her problems and do something different rather than getting high? Instead of additional stress piling up from zoning out on marijuana, she has the wherewithal to tackle her problems head-on and take the initiative to resolve them.

That Big Ol' "Yes, But"

So you think what you have been reading so far makes a lot of sense, but you find yourself occasionally saying, "That may be true for someone else, but it really doesn't apply to me." How often are you ready with a reason why you can't make the changes that someone else is suggesting? Are the words "Yes, but" a frequent part of your vocabulary?

I once heard someone refer to the 'but' in a sentence as a giant eraser. "Yes, I agree. What you are saying is absolutely correct, but I'm now going to disregard (erase) everything you just said."

Like a player in a game of badminton, do you bat away the birdie of solid advice to avoid having to change?

But will you change?

Yes, you're afraid. Yes, it's hard.
Yes, it comes at a cost. Yes, you're worried.
Yes, it's his fault. Yes, she hasn't changed either.
Yes, you're broken, you're empty,
and you're disconnected.
Yes, your therapist hasn't told you how.
Yes, it's an unknown,
and you've never done it before.
Yes, you may fail.
Yes, you're tired of waiting. Yes, it hurts.
Yes, it didn't work the last time you tried it.
Yes, you embarrassed yourself the last time.
Yes, you're afraid you'll end up alone.
Yes, they might laugh at you.
Yes, you'll have to let go.
Yes, then you won't feel in control.
Yes, but...

Won't you say, "Yes, and..."? Yes, I'm sick and tired of being sick and tired. Yes, I want to hope again. Yes, I want to do what is right. Yes, I want to do what works. Yes, I want to live. Yes, I want to change!

Reflection Questions

What would make you sick and tired enough?

What have you been hoping for?

What are you willing to say yes to?

Chapter Eight Power Points

- Get sick and tired enough!
- You'll truly live when you change.
- Doing something different actually works.
- Learn to say, "Yes, and..."

PART THREE

Chapter Nine
The ABCs of Change

So, what is the secret your therapist knows but may not tell you? Are you ready? The secret is that there is no secret. You already have everything you need to make the changes that you desire.

You may lack some information, skills, or preparation, but you can ask for help, get a coach, take a class, or even go see a therapist. Being sick and tired enough and wanting more for your life can serve as a motive or reason to change. And that motivation will put you in a state of readiness and eagerness to change. But what you need, which no one else can give you, is the courage and determination to change.

Because it is hard and scary and comes at a cost, change requires courage and determination. You'll need courage to do something different, despite your fears. You will also need determination and the mental will, tenacity, and persistence to overcome the pain and loss that come with change. The good news is that courage and determination are choices you make in each moment of each day when you are faced with the difficult work of change.

Change Starts with the ABCs

You are the only person who can decide you want to change despite these barriers. No one can make you change, much less make you want to change. And, as I've stated already, I firmly believe some people really don't want to change. Perhaps they never will.

If you are not willing to change or you are not ready to change, accept that. Be content with where you are, because that's exactly where you are going to stay.

But, if you really are ready to change, where do you get the courage and determination or the willingness to do whatever it takes for however long it takes? How do you increase your CQ? Change starts with the ABCs, that is, attention, beliefs, and choices.

Let me give you an example. Monica is having problems on her job. In fact, she's had difficulties with practically every job she's ever worked. She always feels that people don't like her, someone is trying to sabotage her, or they are putting unfair burdens on her.

I asked her to give a specific example of a troubling situation at work. Monica said she worked with a man who had to approve all of her reports before she could submit them. She said this man always "grits his teeth and acts rude," making it hard for her to do her job. Monica was worried the man didn't like her. She was afraid he might get her fired. I asked Monica the following questions.

A: Can you take your focus off this man and instead put your **attention** on doing your job to the best of your ability?

B: Is it possible that this man is not gritting his teeth at all and your perception of him and your **beliefs** about him are inaccurate?

C: Is there some small aspect of your behavior that you can **choose** to do differently?

Her only response was, "Yes, but..." She then proceeded to tell me about the most recent incident where she had asked for a raise, but it was turned down.

I was beginning to suspect that Monica didn't really want to change. It wasn't because she didn't want her life to improve. It was because change is hard and scary and comes at a cost.

I told Monica what I thought her options were:

- She could continue worrying if she preferred, do nothing different, and remain miserable. (She certainly has the perfect right to remain unhappy.)
- She could talk calmly and rationally to this man and/or her boss about her concerns.
- Just in case, she could quietly start looking for another job.
- She could concentrate all of her attention on doing her job well, believe her co-workers like her and accept her and choose to behave accordingly. For example, she could be ready with a smile whenever she encountered this man.

Ideally, you should be able to align your skills, interests, and purpose and express them through your work. Unfortunately, this is not always immediately possible. Right now, you may need your current job. Other work may not be available that would meet your expenses and be deeply gratifying.

Whether it's your job or any other important issues in your life, you've sometimes got to accept that where you are is not where you want to be. For now, this is where you are. You may be in BED.

As you learned in the first part of this book, through the natural course of life, you will get broken, you will feel empty, and you'll become disconnected. While it doesn't feel good as it is happening, these feelings normally subside as your circumstances change and time simply goes by. But, if you find these feelings lingering, it is usually because of a failed solution. Where you've placed your attention, what you believe, or the responses you are choosing have caused you to suffer.

It's important to figure out which BED issue(s) you are dealing with so you can fix what really needs fixing by placing your attention on the right things, examining what you believe, and choosing an appropriate response. Is your problem because you are broken, empty, or disconnected? For example, if you expect your job to fill your emptiness, what happens if, like Monica, you aren't happy with the work you do? You would be trying to fill your emptiness with something that won't work or last.

Sometimes, for the time being, a job is just a job. You will need to have other meaningful pursuits to add joy to your life. If you are dissatisfied with something, let go of your attachment to it as the primary source of your fulfillment in life. If it were truly meant to be your fulfillment, wouldn't it be working? Instead, focus your attention on something different that is more fulfilling. At the same time, you can still do what you can to change it or yourself, if that something is worth changing. Tony did this with his marriage.

I-Witness Testimony: The Most Important Thing to Tony

I made my marriage the most important thing in my life. There's absolutely nothing wrong with that. But when we started having problems, I was left with an emptiness that I didn't know how to fill. When things were good, I was happy and fulfilled. When things were bad, I was unhappy and empty.

I eventually realized that, for me to survive emotionally, I needed to let go of my attachment to my wife as my primary source of happiness (or unhappiness) in life. I took my focus off changing her. Instead, I focused on changing me. I had become a person who I didn't know or like anymore. Not only was I disconnected from my wife, I was disconnected from my true self.

So I put my attention on something meaningful and lasting. For me, that was my relationship with God and the vision I had for myself and my future. I started pursuing goals and dreams I had put off. And

I started volunteering by helping others. Even though things were still bad between me and my wife, I felt restored.

Tony realized his core issue was emptiness. He had tried to fill it with something that was doomed not to last. This failed solution created even more emptiness and suffering in his life. In order to relieve his suffering, he had to do something different. He refocused his attention, changed his beliefs, and made new choices.

May I Have Your Attention, Please: A Is for Attention

Doing something different for a change does not necessarily mean changing your job or spouse, but it always involves changing your focus. Refocusing your attention is the first step in the ABCs of change.

What do you take great pleasure in? What do you enjoy so much that you lose track of time? What are your hobbies? What are you really good at? What do you do or think about that makes you feel proud of yourself? How do you challenge yourself?

Find out what delights you, and put your attention on it. You can't be anxious, depressed, or angry when you are attending to the things you are passionate about. Fill your emptiness with enthusiasm for a healthy activity, goal, or pursuit. Focus your attention on how you feel while engaged in that activity. Rather than concentrating solely on the outcome, that is, its success or failure, get excited about the process. You'll find you are more connected to your true self and your emptiness is filled when you are in touch with your passions.

Uncle Sam Wants You: What Do You Want?

In chapter one, you learned about "being in BED" and how failed solutions lead to suffering. To avoid suffering, you need to fix what really needs fixing. Your failed solutions stem from focusing your attention on fixing the wrong things in the wrong ways.

It is usually easier and always more effective to focus your attention on what you want rather than what you don't want. Let's say you don't want to feel depressed. But how do you not feel depressed? Instead, focus on what you do want. Ask yourself, "When I'm no longer depressed, what will I be thinking, feeling, and doing instead?" Then attend to that. Fix your thoughts on what you want for your relationships, body, or work life. Identify what you are passionate about, and focus on doing more of that. Change will naturally follow.

In chapter two, you learned change is scary because it involves the unknown, unfamiliar, and what-if thinking. Nothing changes when you put your attention on what you fear. In fact, your experience of fear intensifies when it is at the center of your awareness. The more you notice your heart racing and your palms sweating, the more afraid you will become.

For example, if you focus on how afraid you are of changing jobs, you probably won't change jobs. If you focus on how you fear taking a particular risk, you are less likely to take that risk. So what should you focus on instead? Putting your attention on what you would want or do if you weren't afraid gives you the power to change.

The same is true for focusing on what you might lose. Remember, change comes at a cost. Concentrating on what you will lose when you change can become an insurmountable obstacle. Why not turn your attention to and visualize all you will gain when you do something different?

That Crazy Little Thing Called Love

Another effective focus for your attention is giving to someone other than yourself. Psychologists have often observed that helping others increases happiness. When you place your attention on helping others and you become concerned for their well-being, not only does it put your troubles in perspective, it takes your mind off your own fear, pain, and loss. Connecting your heart to another person to compassionately address his or her needs is an effective remedy for healing your brokenness, emptiness, and disconnectedness.

Consider the mother who sees her child in danger. Perhaps he is inches away from being hit by a car in the street or about to be attacked by a rabid dog. Love for her child pushes away any fear she may have. She takes heroic steps to rescue her child from that dangerous situation.

When you encounter a fear that becomes a barrier to change, shift your focus to how your choices might benefit someone else. I did this with my fear of the big slide. When I focused on setting a good example for my kids, I was able to overcome my fear.

Focusing on loving and helping others is very different from filling yourself with a relationship with someone else. This is where Tony went wrong. He erroneously set his focus on using the relationship with his wife, which can wax and wane, to fill his emptiness rather than on the act of giving, serving, and loving, which he can choose to keep consistent. No matter who the person is or how special he or she is, emptiness filled with an ordinary human relationship won't last.

When you instead focus your attention on the things that delight you and that you desire, and fill your heart with love and compassion for others, you will begin to experience peace and change that lasts.

Reflection Questions

What if you already had everything you needed and wanted? What would you spend your time thinking about and wishing for?

Can you put your attention on those things now?

What do you take great pleasure in?

What does your heart desire?

Chapter Nine Power Points

- Courage and determination are choices.
- Change starts with the ABCs: Attention, beliefs, and choices.
- Refocus your attention on the right things.

Chapter Ten
Renew Your Mind

Once you have shifted your attention, sit still and focus on how you are feeling and what you are thinking and why. Then wait. What will you discover? You will begin to tune in to a small voice or gentle whisper that comes from your heart. This inner voice speaks truth and love, which is often in conflict with what you and the rest of the world would generally believe.

The Truth, the Whole Truth, and Nothing But the Truth

What you believe has a tremendous influence on how you feel and what you do. If you believe you are no good and will never amount to anything, it is likely you will feel bad and probably won't accomplish the things you desire in life.

Even if you were horribly abused, some small, but vital part of you will always remain untouched. It is the essence of who you are. If you can focus your attention on that part and allow it to speak, I guarantee that truth will prevail. You can then concentrate on truth rather than the automatic beliefs that you ordinarily hold.

Renewing your mind requires you to reestablish your connection with truth and consciously, deliberately, and lovingly repeat what your heart tells you rather than the negative thought patterns you have believed. Renewing your mind in this way gives you fresh strength and brings life.

If you felt the need to read this book or you've been in therapy, I would guess that your everyday beliefs are largely negative. Being in BED naturally produces pain. We all have negative thoughts occasionally. But, remember, how you interpret and what you do in response to

107

being in BED produces your suffering. Your failed solutions turn into habits. The next thing you know, you are BED-ridden.

Do you have thoughts like these?

"I can't do anything right."

"I'm worthless."

"No one would ever want someone like me."

"I know I'll just make a mess of everything."

These kinds of thoughts are simply not true. Maybe you find it hard to believe the truth about yourself. Over time, you have probably grown accustomed to believing negative things about who you are. The truth is that you are loveable, capable, and acceptable. How do I know this? Believing these things brings life. Believing and acting upon the opposite does not.

Why is it so much easier for you to believe the negative stuff you've been thinking and so much harder to believe something positive? You readily accept critical thoughts without questioning them, so why not try something different? Why not start believing truth without questioning it? If you want, you can always go back to believing the old stuff later! You have nothing to lose except your suffering.

Using brain imaging techniques, neuropsychologists have shown that what you think and believe actually have an effect on your brain and change your neurochemistry. Thoughts, beliefs, and expectations cause the brain to release neurotransmitters that influence your emotions and well-being. So, in addition to cognitive influences, a strong biological mechanism may also be involved in the effect of your thinking on your behavior and emotions.

So fix your thoughts on and believe what is true and lovely. Do this daily and with deliberate, conscious effort. By believing truth, you will experience a shift in thought, emotion, and deed. You (and your brain) will be transformed into an entirely new person simply by changing the way you think.

Fasten Your Belief Belt: The Belt of Truth

Are you careless with your thoughts? Do you let your mind wander wherever it wants to go? It takes a great deal of discipline to take captive those automatic, unconscious thoughts that contradict what truth and love tell you about yourself. The change and transformation you want in your life will result from consistently believing truth and rejecting your negative thoughts. You will need to learn to cultivate more conscious awareness of your thoughts if you want to change them and your behavior.

In addition to the many distractions we face, this is also hard to do because of the pain that sometimes subsequently surfaces. Realizing what you actually believe about yourself, the world around you, and your future is painful. The truth sometimes hurts. But, even when it is painful, ultimately, truth always brings life.

In the previous chapter, you learned how important it is to place your attention on the proper things. Once you identify truth, you must commit to putting your attention on it, letting it soak in, and embracing it. Put truth on like a belt. Make sure it's snug and secure. Let it hold up everything you do.

Early in the Morning: Get on the Right Track

How do you begin your day? Is the TV blaring bad news and distressing images? Have you ever dashed off to work without eating breakfast? How do you think it impacts the rest of your day to start off in the midst of so much confusion?

It takes discipline to focus your attention on the right things and steadily renew your mind by changing what you believe. When you eliminate distractions, especially those that occur first thing in the morning, you will find you are better equipped to make the mental effort required to take authority over your thought-life.

Why not choose to minimize busy distractions like TV, cell phones, and Internet? Of course, I am not suggesting you have to give up these things altogether. But make a note of how much time you spend engaged in these activities and how they impact your thoughts and moods.

We Interrupt This Program ...

Television bombards you with unrealistic messages. It's fitting that TV shows are called "programming." The fantasy world that TV promotes can't help but influence or program what you believe about yourself and your life. What would happen if you cut back on TV viewing for a week? Or, if you are really brave, take a thirty-day fast from TV. In other words, do not watch television for a month. The first time I did it, I felt like I was going through withdrawal and TV was the drug.

I don't think television is inherently evil. After the thirty days are up, I always turn the television back on. But doing the TV fast helps me to readjust my threshold for mindless distractions. I cut back on shows that are really not adding anything positive to my life or beliefs about myself and those around me. After the fast, rather than using television as a tranquilizer or anesthetic, I only watch the shows I actually enjoy.

And Now Back to Our Regularly Scheduled Program

After cutting back, if you discover TV is having little effect on your thought-life, you can always return to watching as much as you like. But why not at least try something different and see what happens? You might discover that your belief belt is easier to put on and keep on. Plus, you have more time to invest in things that would be more productive and conducive to change.

If you want to change, it takes time. Imagine all you could accomplish if you took even half the time you spend with TV, Internet, and idle phone conversations and devoted it to actively pursuing the change you want in your life.

What will you do with all of your extra time once you cut back on these distractions? You could learn a new skill or hobby or cultivate true intimacy and connection with others. Oh, the things you could do if you replaced the time doing something different!

When people do benefit from traditional psychotherapy, I believe it is because the therapy provides a structured opportunity to focus your attention on the issues you are facing and come up with solutions. It is an hour where there are no distractions, you can examine your beliefs, and you can carefully explore your alternatives and choices.

It's Also about the Journey, Not Just the Destination

As a therapist, I always wondered what would happen if you took the one hour a week you might spend in therapy and spent it by yourself, sitting quietly and deliberately reflecting on a particular area of your life. Would you experience just as much change (or even more) for a fraction of the cost? Have you ever done that? When is the last time you sat quietly, meditating on how you wanted something to be different?

Writing in a journal can help you focus your attention and be more aware of your thoughts and beliefs. I've encouraged you to keep a journal as you make your way through this book. You could also journal your journey through life, especially when you are working on a particular issue of change. In addition to the other benefits described in chapter one, journaling provides a venue for sitting quietly and focusing your thoughts.

What will you learn from journaling? You will discover:

- How you are attempting to fix your brokenness
- The things you are trying to fill your emptiness with
- The ways in which you are trying to connect

You will also be able to more clearly see the self-protective patterns of the thoughts, emotions, and behaviors that keep you BED-ridden.

Nothing to Fear but Fear Itself

One theme that often jumps off the pages of a journal is fear. Chapter two explored fear and the role it plays in keeping you from changing. The unknown, unfamiliar, and what-if thinking are all at the root of fear. Fear is not altogether bad, however. Fear is a form of self-protection. It signals danger and it can prevent you from experiencing harm. Nevertheless, fear makes it easy to believe things that really are not true. For example, if you fear that things will turn out badly, you won't take action. But that backfires because you don't know for certain how it will turn out. Will it really be as bad as you predict?

Fear is such an underestimated emotion. It robs you of so much of your power and joy. It debilitates, paralyzes, kills, and destroys. Yet we take it for granted that there will be fear in life. Yes, you should fear certain things, for example, a grizzly bear attacking you, being trapped in a burning building, a stranger approaching in a dark alley with a gun, and so forth. But why fear merely the possibility of things that have yet to happen? Why fear things you can't see and things that are unknown or unfamiliar?

112

There is a big difference between concern and fear. Concern is a legitimate response to a difficult situation or a matter of interest or importance. It will prompt you to carefully examine the issues you are facing. You will explore possible solutions. Then you might evaluate the best alternatives and take action. Concern is productive. Fear, on the other hand, will usually cause you to obsess, avoid, or procrastinate because of the unpleasant experience of dread and anxiety that accompanies it.

While fear has been linked in a positive light to the fight-or-flight response, some scientists also include "freeze and faint." You might become immobilized and incapacitated in the face of fear. When you want to experience change, paralysis is the last thing you need. Concern will prompt you to action. Fear will often bring you to a standstill.

Your true inner self is not fearful; it is powerful, loving, and self-disciplined. You have the ability to control your feelings, overcome your weaknesses, and lovingly pursue what is right despite temptations to do otherwise.

In place of fear and worry, make it a regular practice to clearly identify what you need and be thankful for what you already have. What you need will become clearer as you remove the smoke screen of fear. This clarity brings a peace that will allow you to focus your attention on the things that really matter and are truly pleasing.

As you renew your mind, your tolerance for fear will decline. You will find yourself saying, "I'm sick and tired of fear."

Reflection Question

Think of a situation you would like to change. What do you believe about it?

How have your beliefs been obstacles to achieving the change you want?

What can you think about right now that is true, honorable, right, pure, lovely, admirable, excellent, or praiseworthy?

What could you be doing instead of watching television, checking e-mail, and talking on the phone?

What patterns are you seeing in your journal or these reflection questions?

Chapter Ten Power Points

- What you believe has a tremendous impact on how you feel and what you do.
- Focus on truth and love.
- Overcome the fear in your life.

Chapter Eleven
Change Is a Choice

If you want something different, you have to do something different. Refocusing your attention and renewing your mind and beliefs are the first two steps in the ABCs of change. Feeling and thinking a certain way contribute to change, but lasting change ultimately results only from doing something different.

Therefore, the final step in the ABCs of change requires you to address the C, your choices. This book could just as well be titled *Choose Something Different...For a Change*, emphasizing the role of your free will in experiencing lasting change.

Not only do your choices include your behavior and actions, they also include your thoughts and beliefs. What you choose to pay attention to, think, and believe affects how you feel and impacts what you do.

Where There's Smoke, There's Fire: Follow the Feelings

How will you know when you should choose something different? Let's go back to chapter one. Is your pain out of proportion to your original brokenness? Is your emptiness lingering on longer than you'd like? Do you have negative emotional reactions that are triggered suddenly and unexpectedly? Do you find yourself disconnecting from others in order to protect yourself from being hurt?

Unless you have chosen a response that leads to suffering and/or you believe something other than truth and love, being in BED subsides with time. Your feelings of suffering will help you know if you should choose something different. As you read in chapter seven, feelings serve as a "trail of crumbs" back to your underlying BED issues and failed solutions. You must allow yourself to feel your feelings in order to benefit from them, even though it's hard and scary and comes at a cost. This doesn't mean you feel for feeling's sake. Rather, you can use your pain and negative feelings to help you identify your BED issues and failed solutions. They can also be used as a signal to choose something different.

As you sit still and renew your mind, you might also notice a subtle feeling of discomfort or restlessness. This feeling can signal that you are not where you should be. Don't stay where you are. Don't keep doing what you are doing. Choose something new and different.

Restore Factory Settings: Change What You Do

Once you know you need to choose something different, how will you know what you should do? It's hard for me to talk to you about changing your behavior without also talking about changing your thinking. When you renew your mind and change the way you think, you change who you are. You become a new person. With this transformation, you will have no doubts about what is right, what to do, or how to do it.

In this way, you are like a computer. The software script tells the computer exactly what it should do and in what order, just as your thoughts and beliefs tell you what you should do. If you change the script, you will change what the computer does. Its very nature and purpose will change. If you want your computer to do something different, you write a new script or install new, updated software. If you want to do something different, you have to install new scripts and reprogram your thinking.

118

I was recently reading the instructions for my iPod. One feature allows you to restore factory settings. The instructions caution you prior to using this feature. Restore erases the disk and returns it to its original factory condition. In addition, all software updates and saved songs will be deleted.

Imagine if you could restore your factory settings on the way you think and what you do. What if you could erase all the wrong thinking and untruths you have about yourself? What if you could return to how you thought before you became BED-ridden? Well, you can. The whole process of renewing your mind and choosing something different will change the way you think and show you what you should do.

Necessary But Not Sufficient

In graduate school, we were taught that "insight is necessary but not sufficient for change." I was reminded of this recently as I watched a therapist on a television talk show. The therapist was talking with a guest who had sex with his wife's best friend in his own home. The therapist asked him to identify where in his past he had learned to be so cruel and arrogant. The man tearfully revealed that he learned it from his father.

Everyone applauded. The host called the intervention "brilliant." This was certainly a breakthrough insight for this man. But let me assure you that his insight is not sufficient to change his behavior. Realizing he had learned his selfish, arrogant, and cruel behavior from his dad will not keep him from cheating on his wife in the future. Despite the dramatic and emotional recognition of the origin of his behavior, the tearful acknowledgment is not enough to produce the change he wants in his life. Then what is enough?

119

He will have to choose to want to be someone different and be willing to do something different every day. This will take courage and determination. He'll especially need to be mindful of the A and B in the ABCs of change. For example, where does he focus his attention when he has the urge to cheat? What is he thinking and believing about his wife and his marriage?

Perhaps because it was too painful to actually feel his feelings and let them lead him to his erroneous beliefs, this man started believing a fantasy about how life would be better with his wife's best friend. He tried to fill his emptiness with someone else. He disconnected from his wife and his true feelings.

Instead, he could have focused his attention on what he wanted out of his relationship with his wife and shifted his attention to giving instead of taking. He could have lovingly embraced the truth about himself and his wife and realized his failed solution of infidelity caused him (and her) to suffer. And he could have chosen to do something different, for example, move toward his wife when he felt like pulling away.

Go with the Flow

Change can seem overwhelming.

"I need to change my personality."

"I must change how I do my relationships."

"I need to lose fifty pounds in time for my high school reunion."

My goodness! Those are big tasks. How could you possibly take all that on at once? When you get ready to make a change in your life, you might notice that you begin to feel emotionally overwrought. It may seem like too big of an undertaking.

There are many possible explanations for your apprehension. It is hard. You are afraid of success. You are afraid of failure. Regardless of the explanation, you know you need to do it anyway. How do you resolve this problem? You accept the fact that some days may not go well. Instead of beating yourself up, you go with the flow.

When you get overwhelmed, review what you have previously done. If you have been journaling, go back and read what you have written. Carefully examine it, and write more. This will usually give you insight into what you are feeling and believing and what you should do next. Remember, however, that insight is only the first step.

If you expect to change all at once or in very large chunks, you will probably become frustrated with yourself and give up. Instead, recognize the natural barriers to change: change is hard, scary and comes at a cost. Allow yourself to experience those feelings without giving in to them. When you acknowledge that change is hard and you need patience and perseverance, it makes it easier to accept the small steps that will eventually add up to big steps.

Don't forget you already know and have everything you need to be able to change. You just need to do something different. What you've been doing hasn't been working. So why not try a different approach and see what happens?

The key is listening to truth and trusting the direction that emerges. You may need to be really still before you take that first small step. It may mean being okay with slow, yet steady, progress. But I'm confident that, when you look back, you will be surprised and pleased at just how fast small, steady steps accumulate.

A Lamp for Your Feet and a Light for Your Path

Have you ever driven at night on a country road that did not have any street lamps? If not for the small reflectors on the pavement, you would be unable to see and stay in your own lane. Along your journey of doing something different, there will be times when you are walking on a path that you cannot see. The unknown and unfamiliar are dark and scary.

To keep you from going astray, you will need to create a process or structure that will keep you on track, even when you can't see clearly what is ahead of you. It's like the tracks on a roller coaster. You can go up and down and all around, but the tracks will keep you moving in the right direction.

Have you ever noticed that, when someone plants a new tree, they often put stakes near it and tie the trunk to the stakes? The stakes, made of wood or metal, are driven into the ground to support the small tree and keep it straight while it is still growing. As you are in the process of choosing something different and growing, you will also need to "put up stakes."

It will be important to establish a plan or fixed routine while you are working on change. Set up a schedule of when, where, and how you will refocus your attention and renew your mind. Specifically, determine how you will implement your new choices and behaviors. What will you choose that you will enjoy and be passionate about? What will you do more to replace the things you should do less?

Remember to also regularly set aside time to deliberately meditate on whatever truth and love reveal to you. This is where taking a TV or media fast comes in handy. It frees some of your time and removes a lot of your mental clutter. In the next chapter, I will suggest a few additional options that you might use to help you stay on track.

Reflection Question

Starting today, what is one thing you can choose to do that's different?

What "stakes" can you put in your life that will give you direction and boundaries?

What do you already know? What do you already have?
What can you already do?

Chapter Eleven Power Points

- If you want something different, you have to do something different.
- Put stakes in your life.
- Go with the flow.

Chapter Twelve
Keep the Change

When confronted with the barriers to change, it is helpful to focus on "the n-words": now, next, and new. Ask yourself:

- What am I doing *now*?
- What do I need to do *next*?
- What can I do that's *new*?

Today Is a Gift, and That's Why It's Called the Present: What Am I Doing Now?

By carefully evaluating your current behaviors, you will be able to diagnose which of the three barriers to change you are facing. You should also identify which core BED issues you are dealing with and the negative thoughts you are believing. Sorting this out will help you to select the appropriate strategies to overcome them and avoid your previous failed solutions. In the *now* step, you need to ask yourself the following:

- What am I paying attention to that is counterproductive or distracting?
- What am I believing that is simply not true?
- What choices am I making that are ineffective and bringing stress, chaos, or unrest?
- What am I doing now that I shouldn't be doing?
- What should I be doing now instead?

Focusing on the now also helps you to be in the present. If you are like most people, you spend a lot of time in the past and the future. Regret and rumination result from focusing too much on the past; anxiety and worry result from focusing too much on the future. Staying focused on the now is another stake you can use to stay on track. The only time you actually have is right now. The only place you can have a direct impact on your life is the present.

Don't Ignore the Small Stuff: What Do I Need To Do Next?

Once you have evaluated your current beliefs and behaviors, you will need to identify what you should do *next*. It is usually apparent what the next, small step should be that will move you toward your desired outcome. Now is not the time to take a giant leap. Instead, take a small step in the right direction.

Don't sweat the small stuff. But do focus on the small stuff. In order to change, you must choose daily each little thing that you will do differently. It may only need to be one little thing. It could be several, but it should not be too many. Whatever it is, it should be small and doable. Choose the next small thing that you are able to do that will put you closer to where you ultimately want to be.

In chapter five, you learned that psychologists suggest that doing something for twenty-one days makes it a habit. Try focusing on one small thing for three weeks before you move on to the next small thing. That small thing could be replacing a particular negative thought about your physical appearance with a more positive statement. Or it could be smoking one less cigarette every other day. Also remember, it is more effective to focus on what you want and the small things you will do in place of the undesirable things.

Be aware that the next step is not always sequential or logical. Sometimes, the next small step is something you wouldn't expect to come after the previous step. For example, when writing this book, I jumped around out of order and did not write beginning to end in a logical sequence. The next sentence or paragraph was not always the "next" sentence or paragraph. Be willing to be flexible.

Do Something Different for a Change: What Can I Do That's New?

The next step after the *next* step is the *new* step. Herein lies the main point of this book. What you've been doing in the past is the very thing that has led you to where you are. What you've been doing in the past is the very thing that has gotten you stuck. What you've been doing in the past is the very reason you must now do something new and different to end up somewhere other than where you are. Doing more of the same only gets you more of the same.

The only way to experience a change is to do something new. Something new is generally regarded as better than the old. It reinvigorates, restores, and revives. It is often unfamiliar and strange. You may be inexperienced with it or unaccustomed to it, but don't let that discourage you from trying it.

No Comparison: Run the Race That's Marked Out for You

You can learn a lot about change by studying athletes. Athletes train. Each day, they choose to do the little things repeatedly in their pursuit of excellence. They condition themselves mentally and physically. They work hard. They sweat. They sometimes lose, but they always get back in the game.

One thing I can assure you is that you will not change if you do not do the work. You can desire change all you want, but, as you've seen throughout this book, you must be willing to do what's required to achieve that change. You have to keep your mind focused on what you need to do. You have to persevere. You have to take responsibility.

127

You have to be willing to do whatever it takes. If you take your eyes off the mark, you will lose.

Athletes provide you with a wonderful model of the hard work that change requires, but the metaphor is flawed. Sports involve competition. And competition results in comparison. Nothing will discourage you and hinder your change more quickly than comparing yourself and your progress to others. There will always be someone faster, stronger, and better than you.

In my triathlon experience, I have accepted that I will probably never be a blue ribbon, first-place finisher. In the swimming leg of my very first triathlon, I came in 2,215 out of 2,307 participants. This means I swam faster than only ninety-two people. But I did not drown, so I was quite happy with this first-time achievement.

At this writing, I am one week away from my second triathlon. Over the course of my training this year, I have taken six minutes off my time. That is probably still not enough to jump all the way up to first place, but it is a significant change in my performance due to my effort.

If I were measuring my success against everyone else's performance, I would be sadly disappointed. But I am measuring my success relative to my own improvement and effort. I am doing better than I was doing before, so I have succeeded.

Press on and run hard to reach the end of your race, not someone else's. Anne learned this lesson one summer afternoon.

I-Witness Testimony: Anne Tries the Jet Ski

I can't remember his name, but a friend of my boyfriend came to town, pulling two Jet Skis on a small trailer. We all went out to the beach for a day of fun in the sun, but I was afraid to get on the Jet Ski and ride. After watching everyone have such a good time, I decided I would put my fear aside and try it.

The friend explained I would have to start from a standing position in the water and then begin to accelerate. Then I should pull myself up onto the Jet Ski. If it wasn't moving fast enough before I got on, it would tip over. Unfortunately, I didn't have enough upper body strength to pull myself up while it was moving forward. When I slowed down, it would tip over. When I sped up, it dragged me.

I tried repeatedly. My arms were sore, and my legs were bruised from hitting the back of the Jet Ski. I finally gave up. But, much to my surprise, I wasn't disappointed. I was so proud of myself for trying something scary and terribly difficult. Even though I wasn't able to ride the Jet Ski like everyone else, I felt good about myself for being willing to try.

Resisting the urge to compare yourself to others will help keep your change on track and result in lasting change. In addition, you'll have the opportunity to feel good about what you've accomplished, regardless of how it measures up to what someone else may have done.

Right On: Doing What's Right

Finally, when choosing something different, be sure to also choose what is right. I think this is such an important part of experiencing lasting change that I want to discuss it again here.

When you start evaluating your choices and decide to choose something different, make sure it is something right, not just something pleasurable or easy. Beware of shortcuts, unethical options, and outright illegal actions. As you read in chapter eight, doing what's right keeps you safe. It helps you feel good about yourself, and it works.

If you are doing what you need to be doing, nothing more and nothing less, you don't have to worry. This becomes another stake to help keep you on the right track. Even if things don't work out as you wished, at least you

129

know you did what was right. You'll have no regrets, and you'll be above reproach.

Accountability: The "Other" A

Are you in trouble? Are you suffering? You should confide in an honest, genuine friend. Talk to him or her about what you are struggling with. The support, encouragement, and confidence of a trustworthy friend are powerful and produce lasting results. A friend to whom you are accountable helps you to choose what's right.

Your friend cannot make the change happen for you, but his or her acceptance of you helps to heal the experience of guilt and shame that your past behavior caused. He or she can also vouch for you when others don't believe that your transformation is real. Accountability is another stake you can put up. Having just one other person who is on your side and can remind you of the new choices you've committed to executing is invaluable in helping you to grow and stay on track.

Beware, however. You may end up with just that one accountability partner. In chapter four, you discovered that change comes at a cost. You may lose friends who don't want you to change because they themselves are not willing to change. If you are fortunate to have at least one person stick around and cheer you on while you change, hold onto him or her. Remember, you may need to stand alone while you are going through the change process. You can't always be guaranteed a support person. And you cannot use one's absence as an excuse not to change.

Boldness: The "Other" B

There comes a point where you must simply start doing what you need to do and stop doing what you need to stop. You have to be bold. Boldness involves an ability to take risks while remaining confident and courageous. Remember, not everyone really wants to change. You must decide that you do. Then you must commit yourself to change, be willing to do whatever it takes, and boldly step to the challenge.

Consequences: The "Other" C

There are always natural consequences to our choices. Some are good; some are bad. What you do and don't do will always have consequences, some now and some later. These consequences affect you and others. This is a law of nature. If you focus your attention on the consequences of your choices, it will shape your actions. Are you getting the results you want? If not, you can make adjustments and take a small, new step towards change.

Earlier, you learned to focus on the process and enjoyment of a pursuit or passion rather than performance-based outcomes. Your self-esteem is enhanced when, among other things, you focus on your effort rather than solely on actual performance. You also learned how comparing your performance to others is especially damaging. Please understand the difference between attending to the consequences of your choices and over-attending to the outcomes of your performance.

If what you choose yields desirable consequences, your choices are automatically strengthened through the mechanism that psychologists call "positive reinforcement." Focusing on the positive consequences of your choices will stimulate your interest and enthusiasm for making similar choices in the future.

The Inside Scoop

So now you know the ABCs of change. You must refocus your attention, change your beliefs, and make new choices. You also now know what your therapist knows even though he or she may not have told you:

- There is no secret.
- You are suffering because of your previous, failed attempts to address your pain.
- Change is hard and scary and will cost you some things you don't want to give up. But you still can do it anyway!
- You need to be satisfied with what you have while working on what you want.
- It isn't anyone else's fault, including your spouse, parents, kids, or boss that you haven't changed.
- Only you can decide that you are sick and tired of being sick and tired.
- It's not enough to simply want to change. You have to be willing to do whatever it takes to change.
- Fear is probably the biggest barrier you will need to overcome in order to change.
- You are choosing the very things that cause your own suffering.
- Doing what is right, ethical, and legal is very important when it comes to change.

Obviously, all of this knowledge is not enough to produce the change you want in your life. Ultimately, after you refocus your attention and change your beliefs, you must still do something different. And only you can exercise the courage and determination needed to produce lasting change in your life.

Some people are knowledge junkies. They love being "in the know." They want to have information that no one else is privy to. But where does that information get you if you don't apply it and put it into action? You can talk about your problems. You can obtain good information and even come up with a solution. But, ultimately, knowledge without action is a dead end. I want to encourage you to bring your knowledge to life by putting what you've learned here to work.

Staying on Track

At the age of forty-two, I got braces for the second time. I wore braces the first time when I was in junior high school. My teeth straightened out pretty quickly, and the braces were replaced with a retainer. I took the retainer off whenever I ate. One day at school, I accidentally threw it away with my lunch tray.

Unfortunately, I never mentioned to my mother that I had lost my retainer. My teeth gradually shifted. Over time, they actually got worse than what they were before my braces. Many years later, my dentist recommended that I wear braces again.

As an adult, your teeth move more slowly. It costs more money. And it hurts. Without a retainer, given enough time, your teeth will shift back to their previous positions. I can assure you this time I won't lose my retainer.

The same is true with change. You must keep a structure in place to maintain the change you've achieved. The older you get, the more difficult it becomes. It's hard and it comes at a cost, but I'd like to persuade you that it's worth it. What will you do to stay on track? I challenge you to do something different and keep the change!

Reflection Question

What one small new thing can you do in place of one small thing you are currently doing?

Who are you accountable to?

What do you need to be bold about and just do?

What desirable consequences do you experience when you do something different?

What do you now know that you need to put into action?

What will keep you from doing what you know?

Will you do it anyway?

Chapter Twelve Power Points

- Remember to ask yourself, "What now? What next? What new?"
- Focus on your own effort and improvement.
- Remember the "other" ABCs: accountability, boldness, and consequences.
- Put your knowledge into action.
- Do something different...and keep the change!

Epilogue

Let's see. We left off with me "up in a tree," feeling deeply unhappy, unfulfilled, and alone. When I realized I was even up in a tree, I believed that feeling broken, empty, and disconnected was totally due to the problems in my marriage. Sometime later, however, I discovered I was broken, empty, and disconnected before I even met my husband.

My strong desire to get married and have a family in the first place was my failed solution to being in BED. When my marriage went bad, I reasoned that, if I could just fix it, I would get out of BED. I was focusing my attention on the wrong things.

What I didn't realize at the time was that I had to go back and examine my core BED issues, what I believed about them, and what I did in response that caused my suffering. I had to embrace my brokenness, touch my emptiness, and acknowledge how disconnected I was to see my negative beliefs and responses clearly. This was profoundly painful and the reason why I hadn't done it any sooner. Truly experiencing the pain of being in BED was hard and scary. It cost me, but I eventually did it.

Through quiet reflection, journaling, and, yes, even some psychotherapy, I learned my suffering was primarily due to erroneous beliefs and fears about abandonment and ending up alone. How ironic that my solutions got me, to some degree, the very things I feared.

I also had issues around not feeling good enough. At the time, I didn't realize what a dead-end the comparison game was. I now realize there will always be someone more _____ (fill in the blank) than me. And that's perfectly okay.

139

Applying the ABCs, I refocused my attention, changed my beliefs, and, subsequently, chose something different. It took time and hard work. Eventually, however, my emotional pain and emptiness were healed, my broken heart was restored, and I experienced lasting change. In the midst of my transformation, I wrote this book as a gift to you. It is my sincere wish that what I've written will inspire you, too, to do something different for a change!

About the Author

Dr. Peggy Mitchell Norwood is a clinical psychologist and professor of psychology. Prior to her teaching career, which has spanned over ten years in Virginia and Colorado, Dr. Peg worked as a psychotherapist in a variety of inpatient and outpatient mental health settings.

Currently the host of the television talk show, "Perspectives," she teaches psychology at the Community College of Aurora and University of Colorado, Denver.

Dr. Peg lives in Denver with her teenaged twins, Ali and Richard and enjoys cooking, swimming, biking, walking, and competing in triathlons. A graduate of Brown University and the University of Virginia, she is also an ordained teacher with Global Change Network, USA.

This is her first book.

I would love to hear from you!

You can write me at

drpeg@hotmail.com

or visit

www.DrPegOnline.com

18650773R00077

Made in the USA
Charleston, SC
14 April 2013